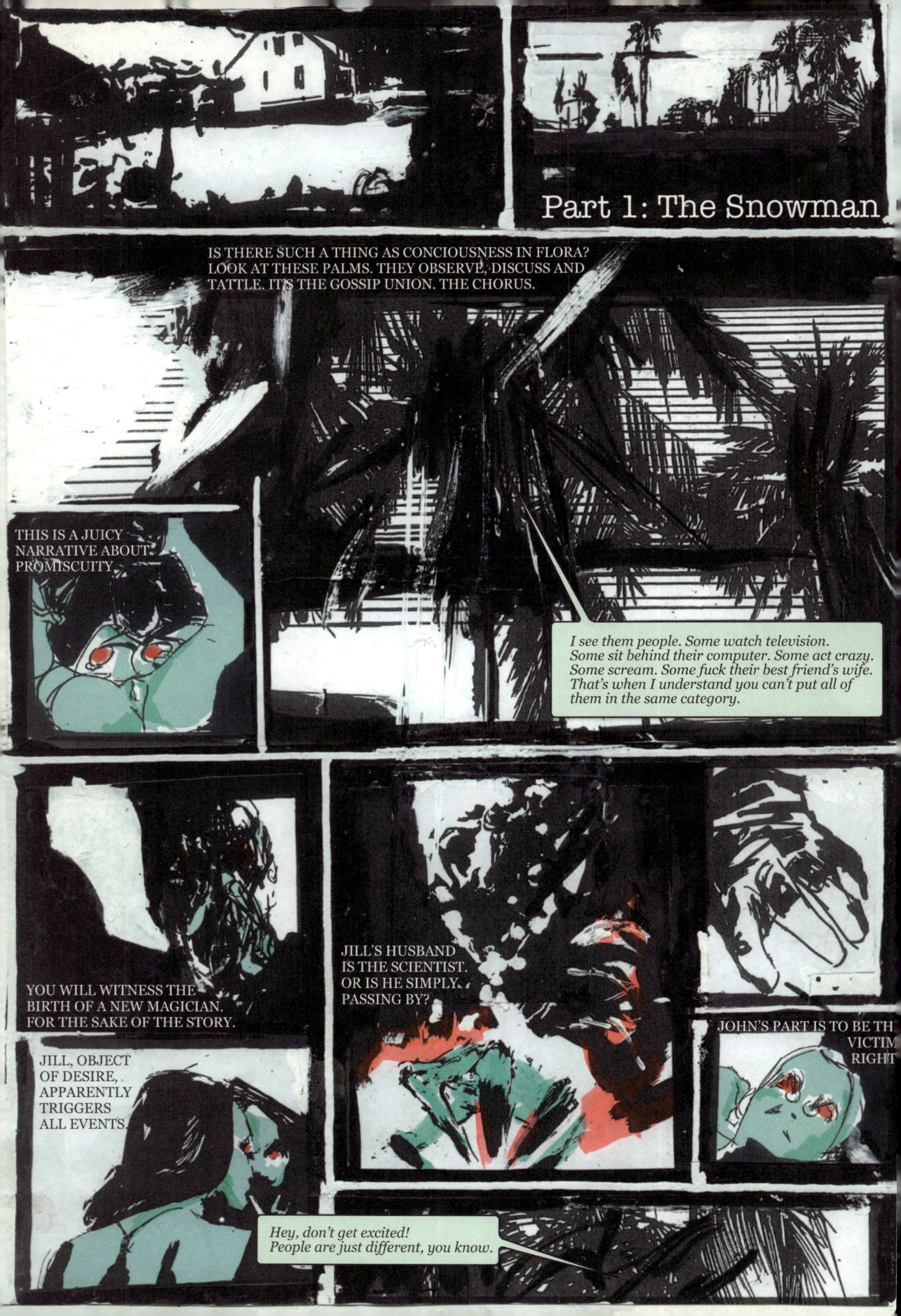

Part 1: The Snowman
IS THERE SUCH A THING AS CONCIOUSNESS IN FLORA? LOOK AT THESE PALMS. THEY OBSERVE, DISCUSS AND TATTLE. IT'S THE GOSSIP UNION. THE CHORUS.
THIS IS A JUICY NARRATIVE ABOUT PROMISCUITY
I see them people. Some watch television. Some sit behind their computer. Some act crazy. Some scream. Some fuck their best friend's wife. That's when I understand you can't put all of them in the same category.
YOU WILL WITNESS THE BIRTH OF A NEW MAGICIAN. FOR THE SAKE OF THE STORY.
JILL'S HUSBAND IS THE SCIENTIST. OR IS HE SIMPLY PASSING BY?
JOHN'S PART IS TO BE TH VICTIM RIGHT
JILL, OBJECT OF DESIRE, APPARENTLY TRIGGERS ALL EVENTS.
Hey, don't get excited! People are just different, you know.

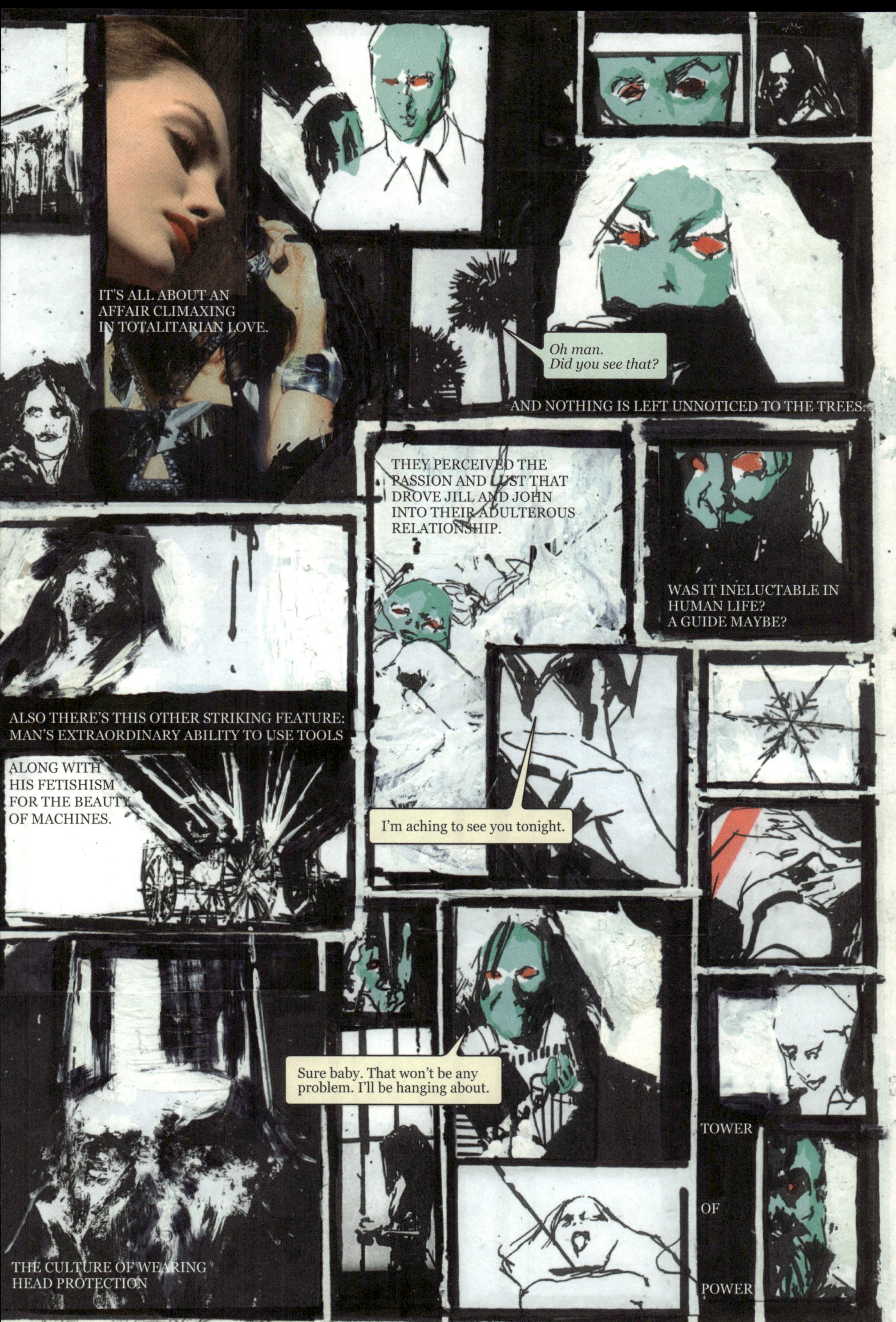

IT'S ALL ABOUT AN AFFAIR CLIMAXING IN TOTALITARIAN LOVE.
Oh man.
Did you see that?
AND NOTHING IS LEFT UNNOTICED TO THE TREES.
THEY PERCEIVED THE PASSION AND LUST THAT DROVE JILL AND JOHN INTO THEIR ADULTEROUS RELATIONSHIP.
WAS IT INELUCTABLE IN HUMAN LIFE?
A GUIDE MAYBE?
ALSO THERE'S THIS OTHER STRIKING FEATURE: MAN'S EXTRAORDINARY ABILITY TO USE TOOLS
ALONG WITH HIS FETISHISM FOR THE BEAUTY OF MACHINES.
I'm aching to see you tonight.
Sure baby. That won't be any problem. I'll be hanging about.
TOWER
OF
POWER
THE CULTURE OF WEARING HEAD PROTECTION

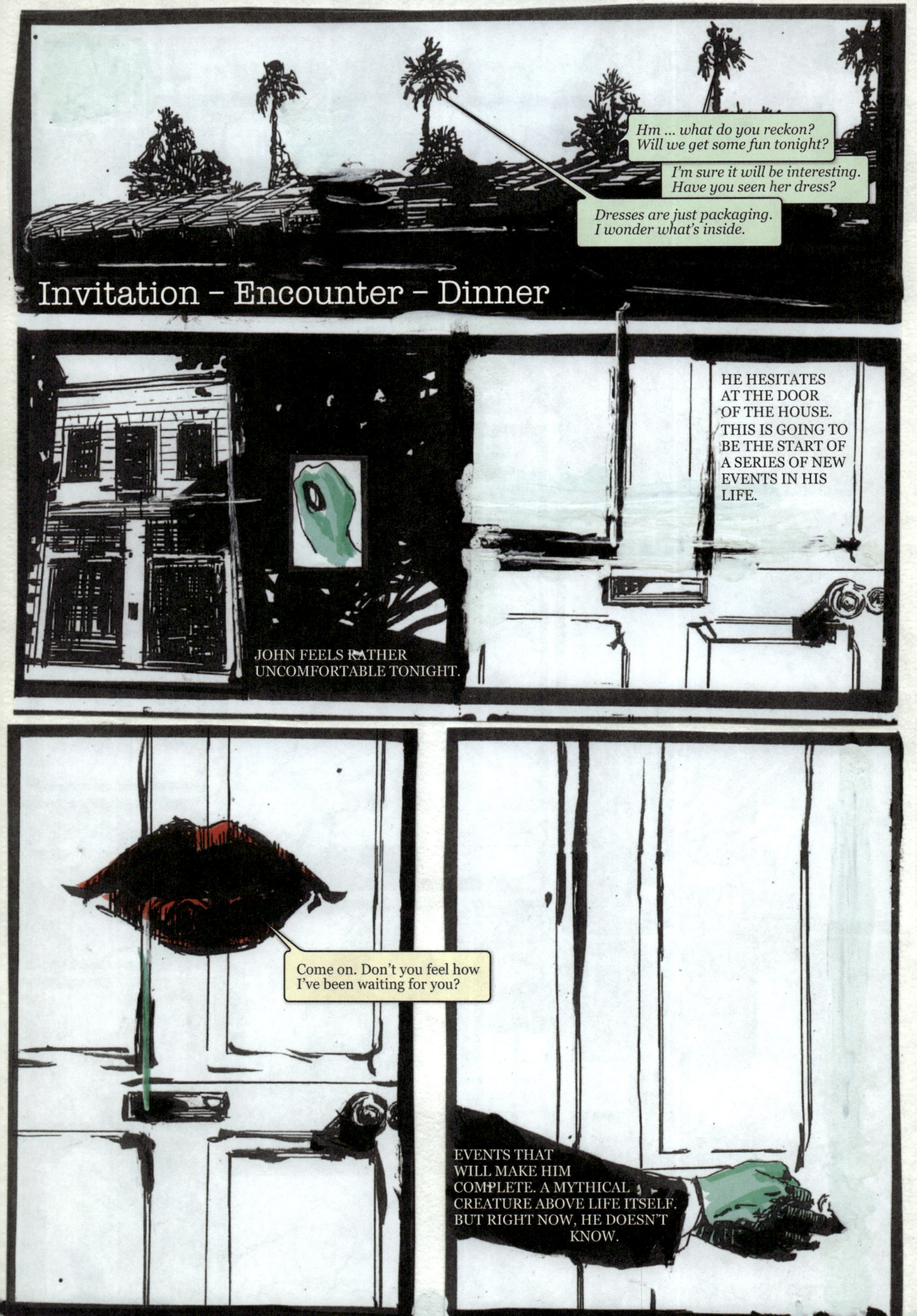

Invitation – Encounter – Dinner

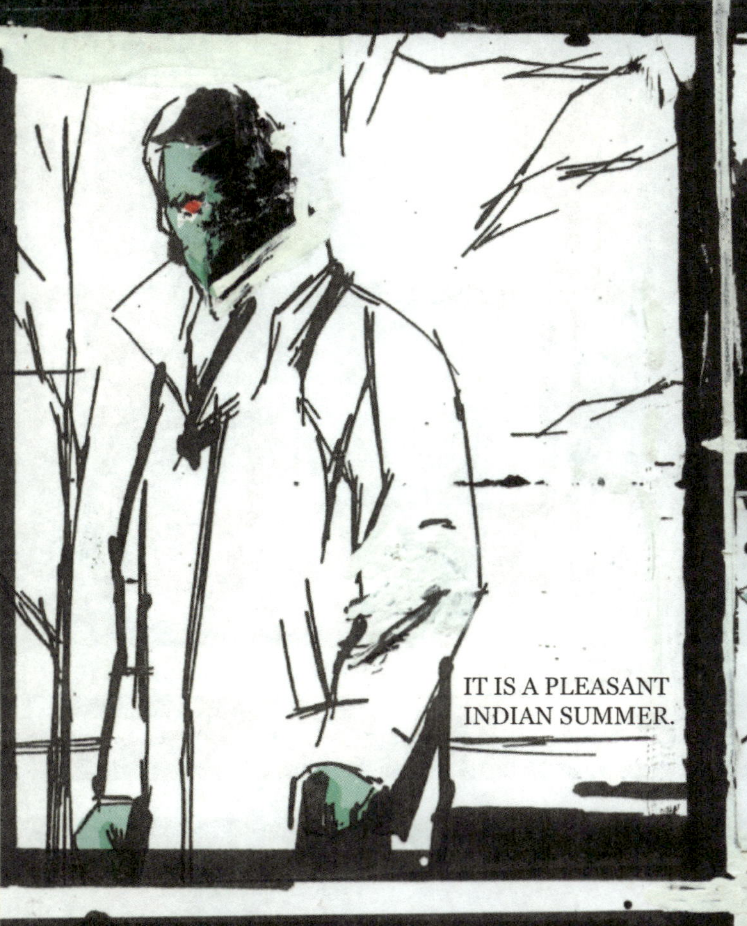

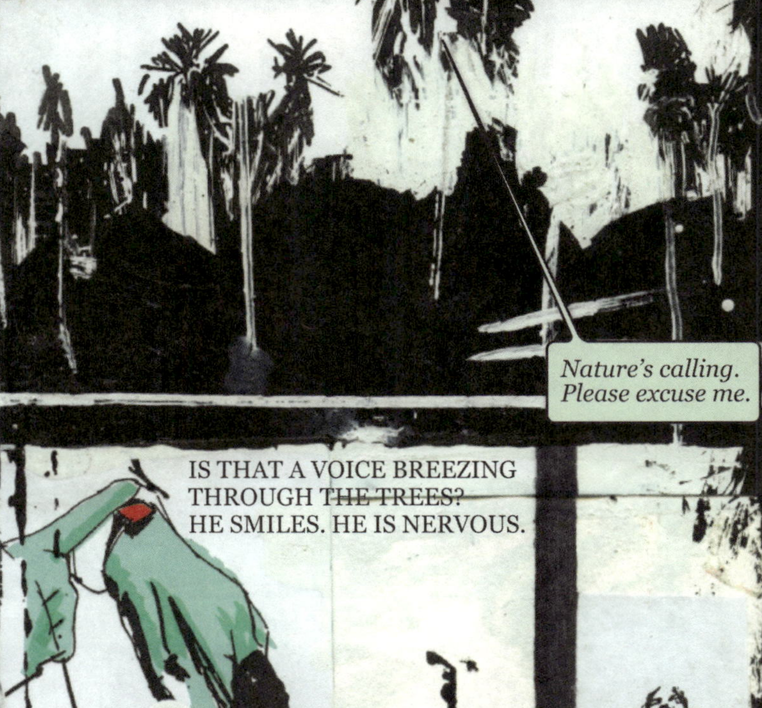

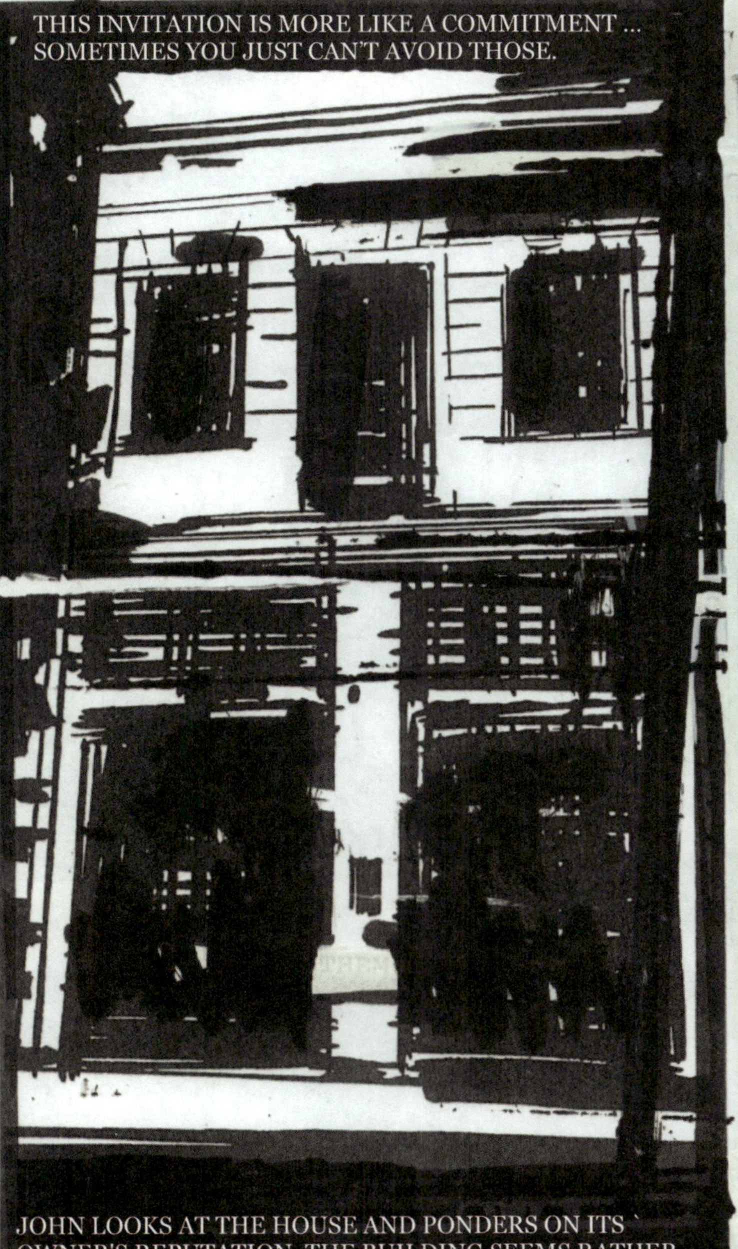

JOHN LOOKS AT THE HOUSE AND PONDERS ON ITS OWNER'S REPUTATION. THE BUILDING SEEMS RATHER SMALL ACTUALLY.

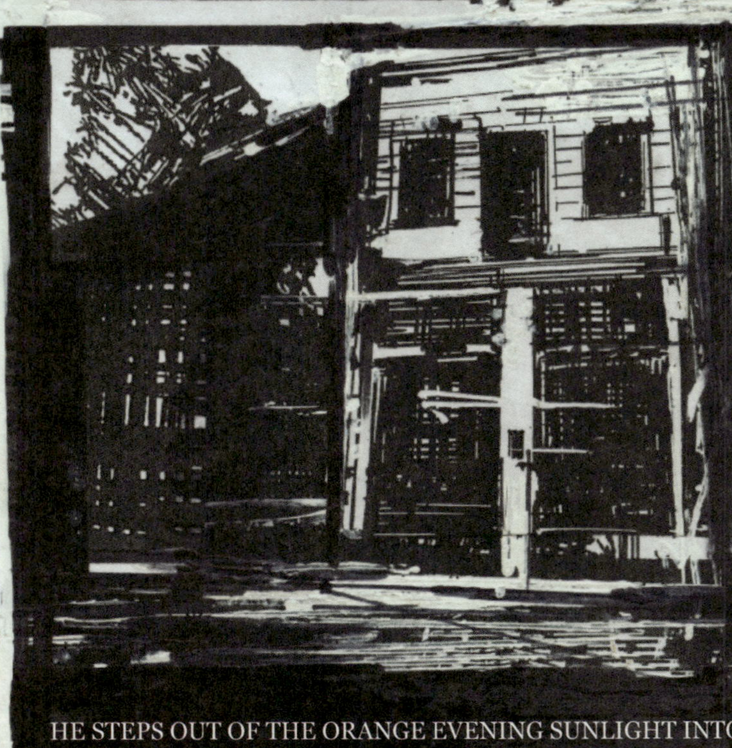

HE STEPS OUT OF THE ORANGE EVENING SUNLIGHT INTO THE DUSKY HALLWAY.

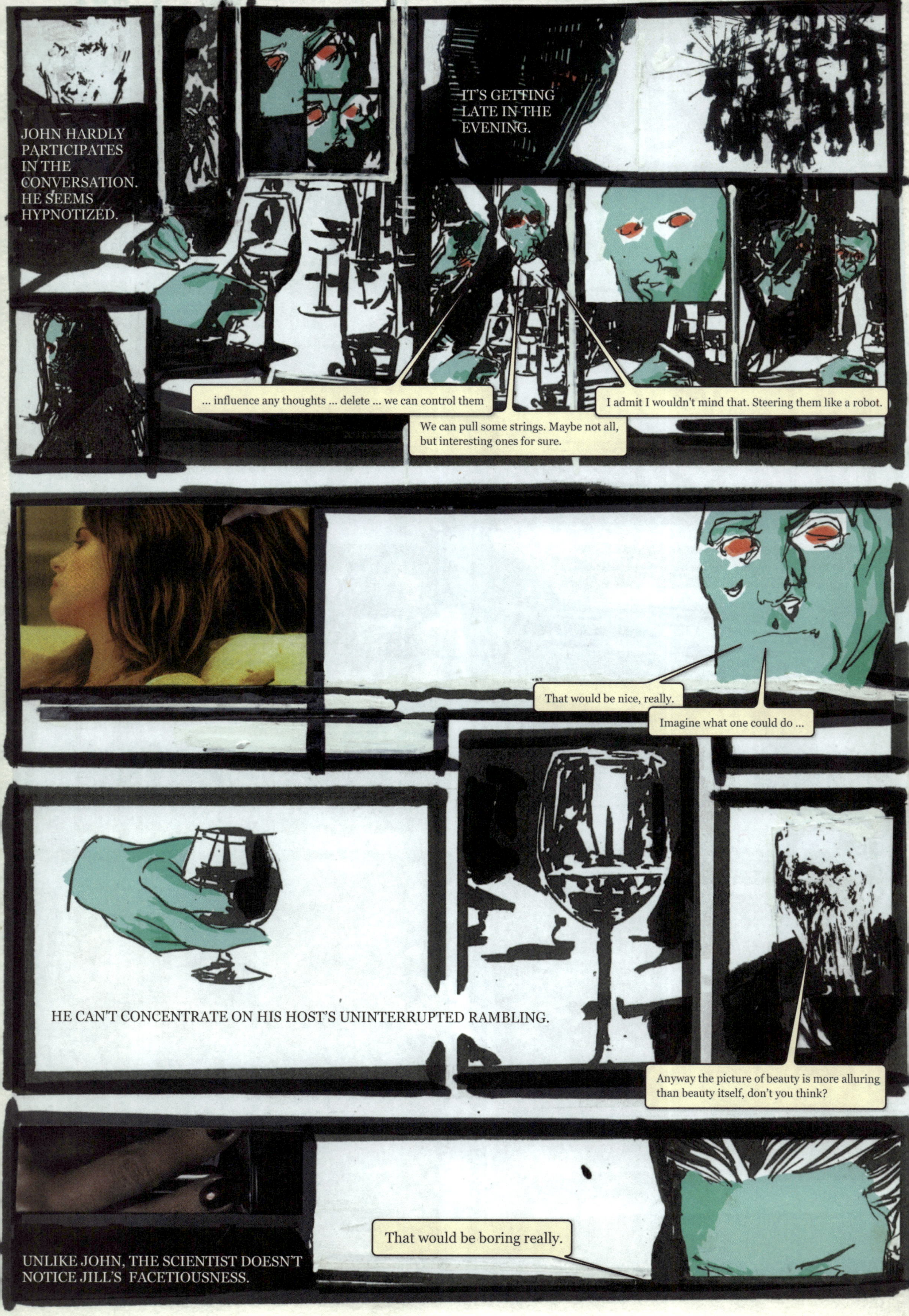

JOHN HARDLY PARTICIPATES IN THE CONVERSATION. HE SEEMS HYPNOTIZED.
IT'S GETTING LATE IN THE EVENING.
... influence any thoughts ... delete ... we can control them
We can pull some strings. Maybe not all, but interesting ones for sure.
I admit I wouldn't mind that. Steering them like a robot.
That would be nice, really.
Imagine what one could do ...
HE CAN'T CONCENTRATE ON HIS HOST'S UNINTERRUPTED RAMBLING.
Anyway the picture of beauty is more alluring than beauty itself, don't you think?
That would be boring really.
UNLIKE JOHN, THE SCIENTIST DOESN'T NOTICE JILL'S FACETIOUSNESS.

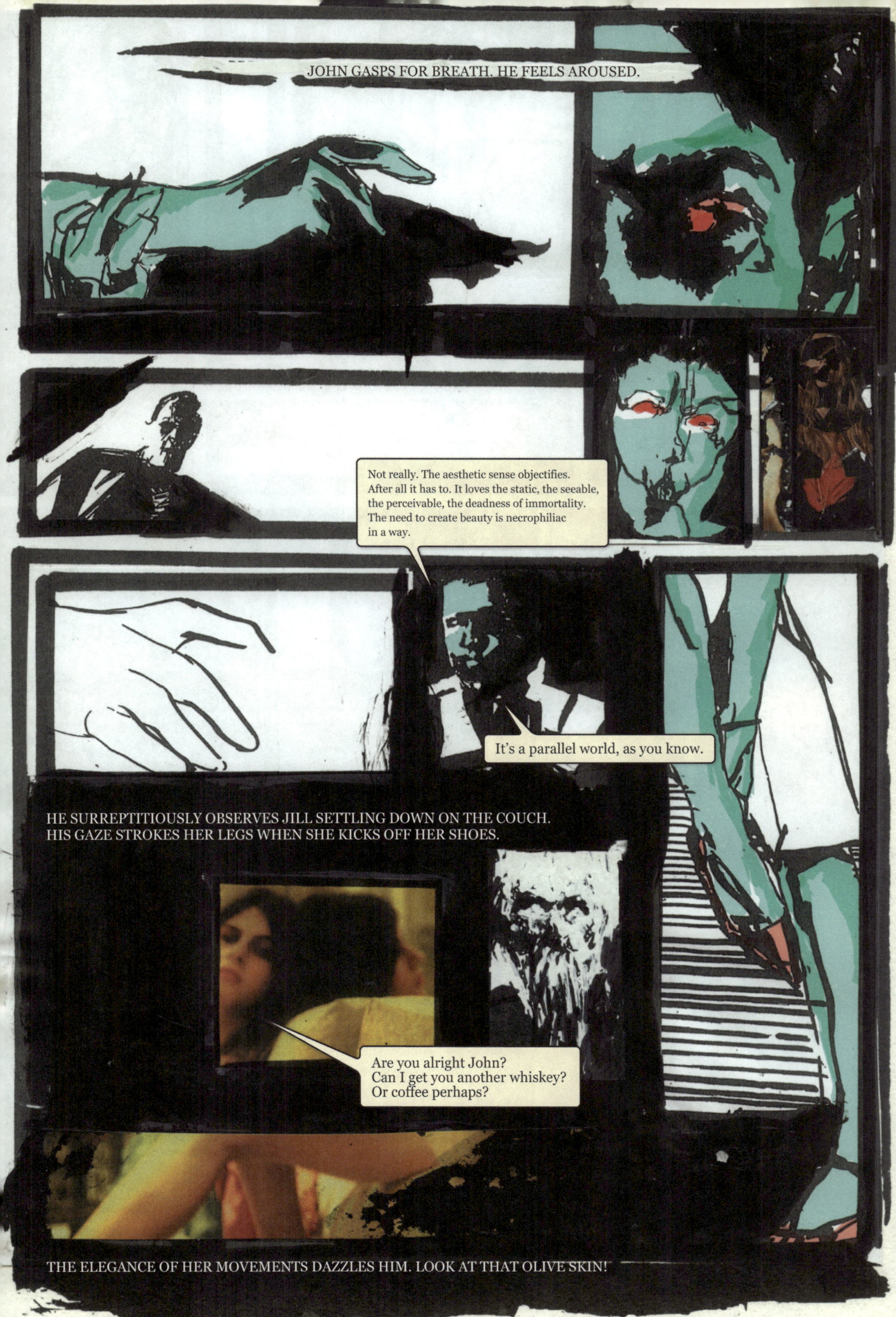

JOHN GASPS FOR BREATH. HE FEELS AROUSED.
Not really. The aesthetic sense objectifies. After all it has to. It loves the static, the seeable, the perceivable, the deadness of immortality. The need to create beauty is necrophiliac in a way.
It's a parallel world, as you know.
HE SURREPTITIOUSLY OBSERVES JILL SETTLING DOWN ON THE COUCH. HIS GAZE STROKES HER LEGS WHEN SHE KICKS OFF HER SHOES.
Are you alright John? Can I get you another whiskey? Or coffee perhaps?
THE ELEGANCE OF HER MOVEMENTS DAZZLES HIM. LOOK AT THAT OLIVE SKIN!

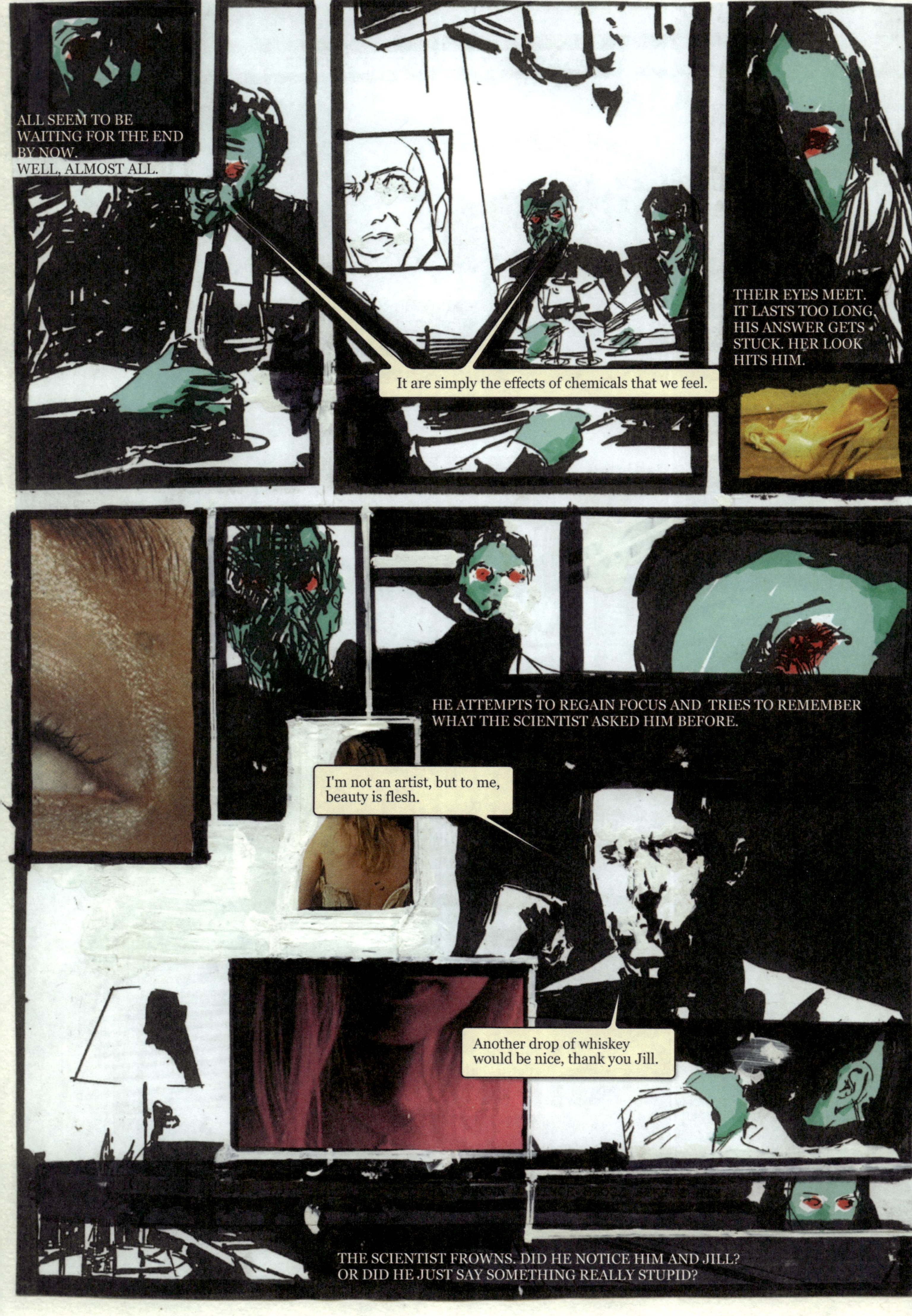

ALL SEEM TO BE WAITING FOR THE END BY NOW. WELL, ALMOST ALL.
It are simply the effects of chemicals that we feel.
THEIR EYES MEET. IT LASTS TOO LONG. HIS ANSWER GETS STUCK. HER LOOK HITS HIM.
HE ATTEMPTS TO REGAIN FOCUS AND TRIES TO REMEMBER WHAT THE SCIENTIST ASKED HIM BEFORE.
I'm not an artist, but to me, beauty is flesh.
Another drop of whiskey would be nice, thank you Jill.
THE SCIENTIST FROWNS. DID HE NOTICE HIM AND JILL? OR DID HE JUST SAY SOMETHING REALLY STUPID?

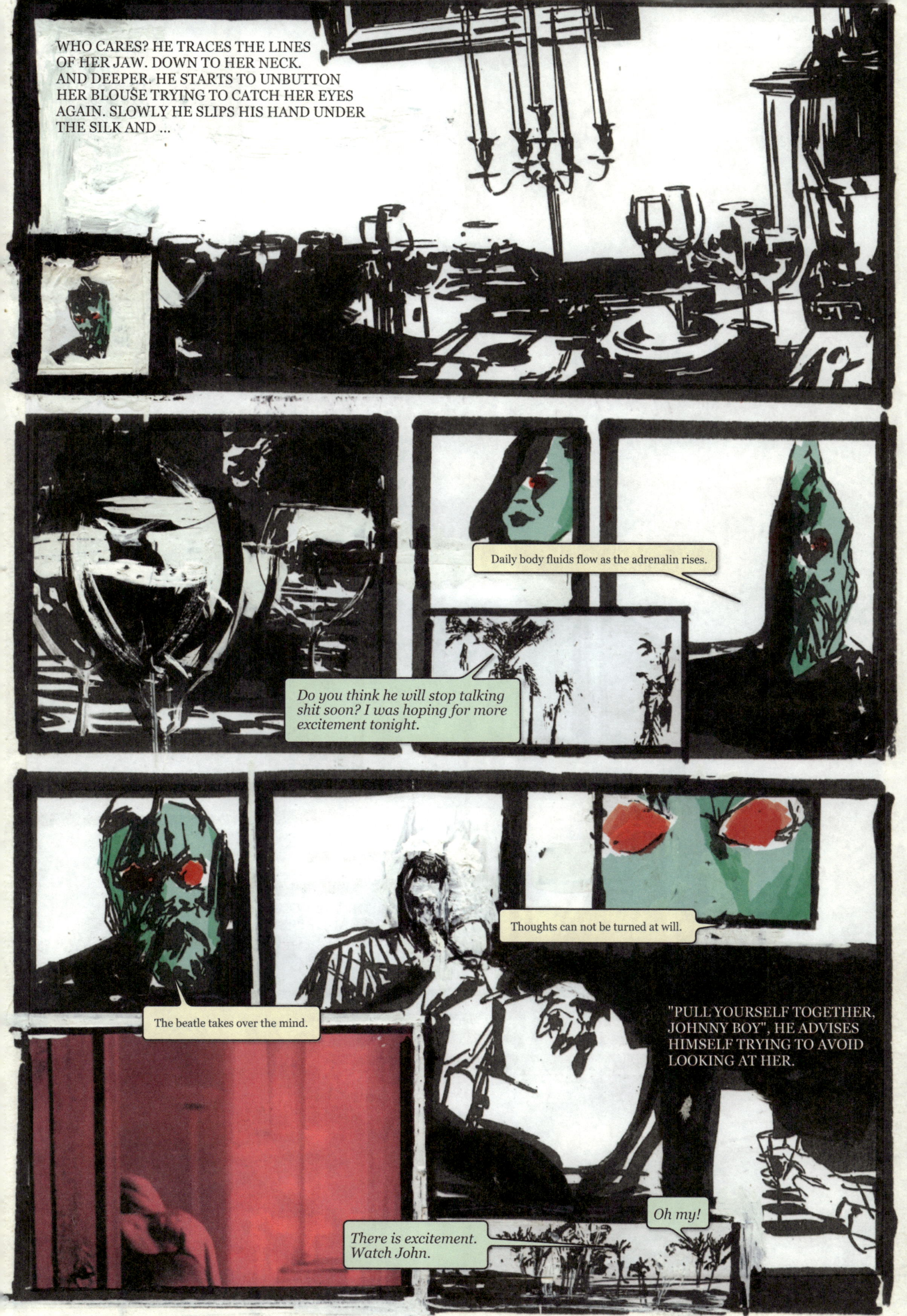

WHO CARES? HE TRACES THE LINES OF HER JAW. DOWN TO HER NECK. AND DEEPER. HE STARTS TO UNBUTTON HER BLOUSE TRYING TO CATCH HER EYES AGAIN. SLOWLY HE SLIPS HIS HAND UNDER THE SILK AND ...
Daily body fluids flow as the adrenalin rises.
Do you think he will stop talking shit soon? I was hoping for more excitement tonight.
Thoughts can not be turned at will.
The beatle takes over the mind.
"PULL YOURSELF TOGETHER, JOHNNY BOY", HE ADVISES HIMSELF TRYING TO AVOID LOOKING AT HER.
Oh my!
There is excitement. Watch John.

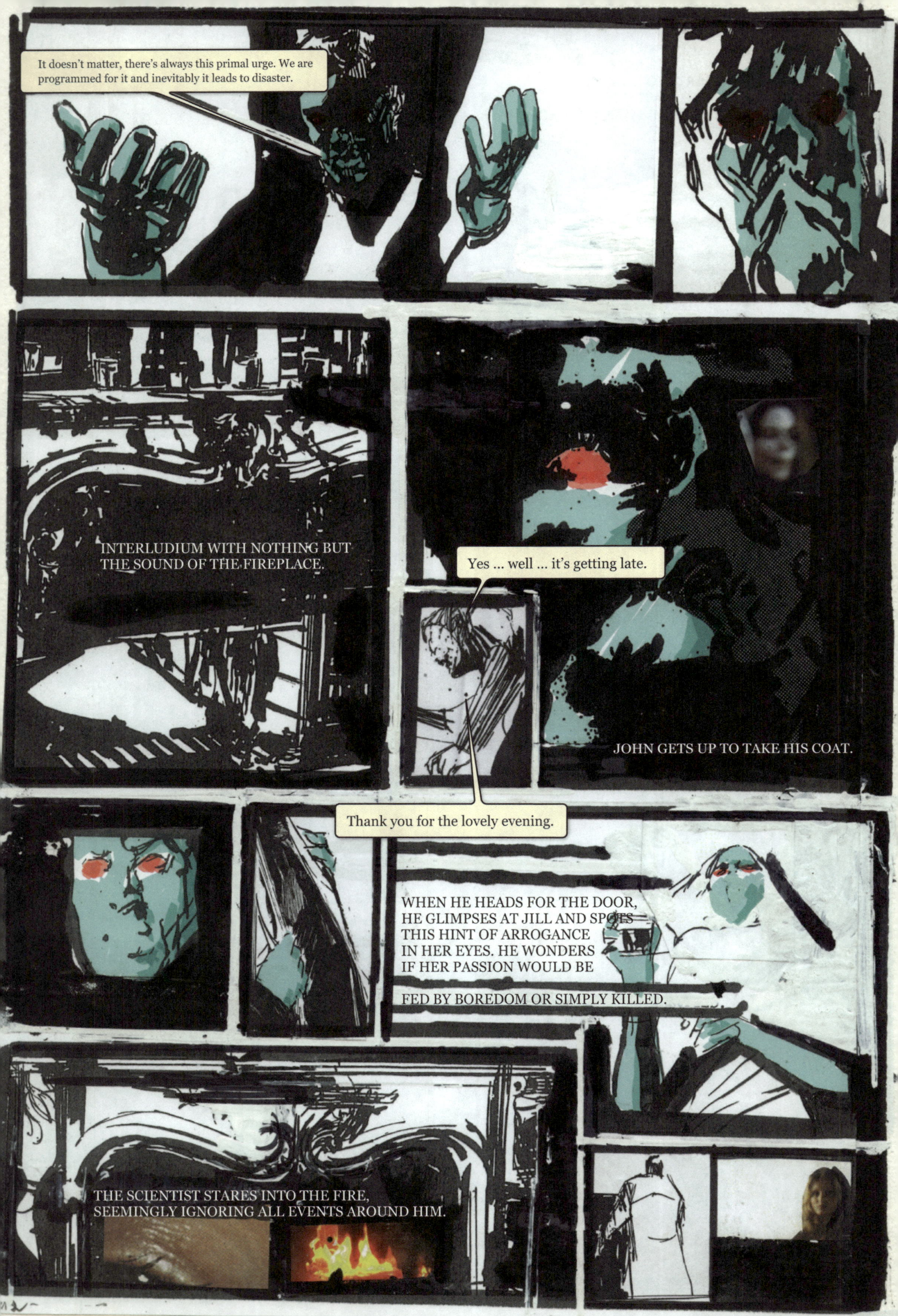

It doesn't matter, there's always this primal urge. We are programmed for it and inevitably it leads to disaster.
INTERLUDIUM WITH NOTHING BUT THE SOUND OF THE FIREPLACE.
Yes ... well ... it's getting late.
JOHN GETS UP TO TAKE HIS COAT.
Thank you for the lovely evening.
WHEN HE HEADS FOR THE DOOR, HE GLIMPSES AT JILL AND SPOTS THIS HINT OF ARROGANCE IN HER EYES. HE WONDERS IF HER PASSION WOULD BE
FED BY BOREDOM OR SIMPLY KILLED.
THE SCIENTIST STARES INTO THE FIRE, SEEMINGLY IGNORING ALL EVENTS AROUND HIM.

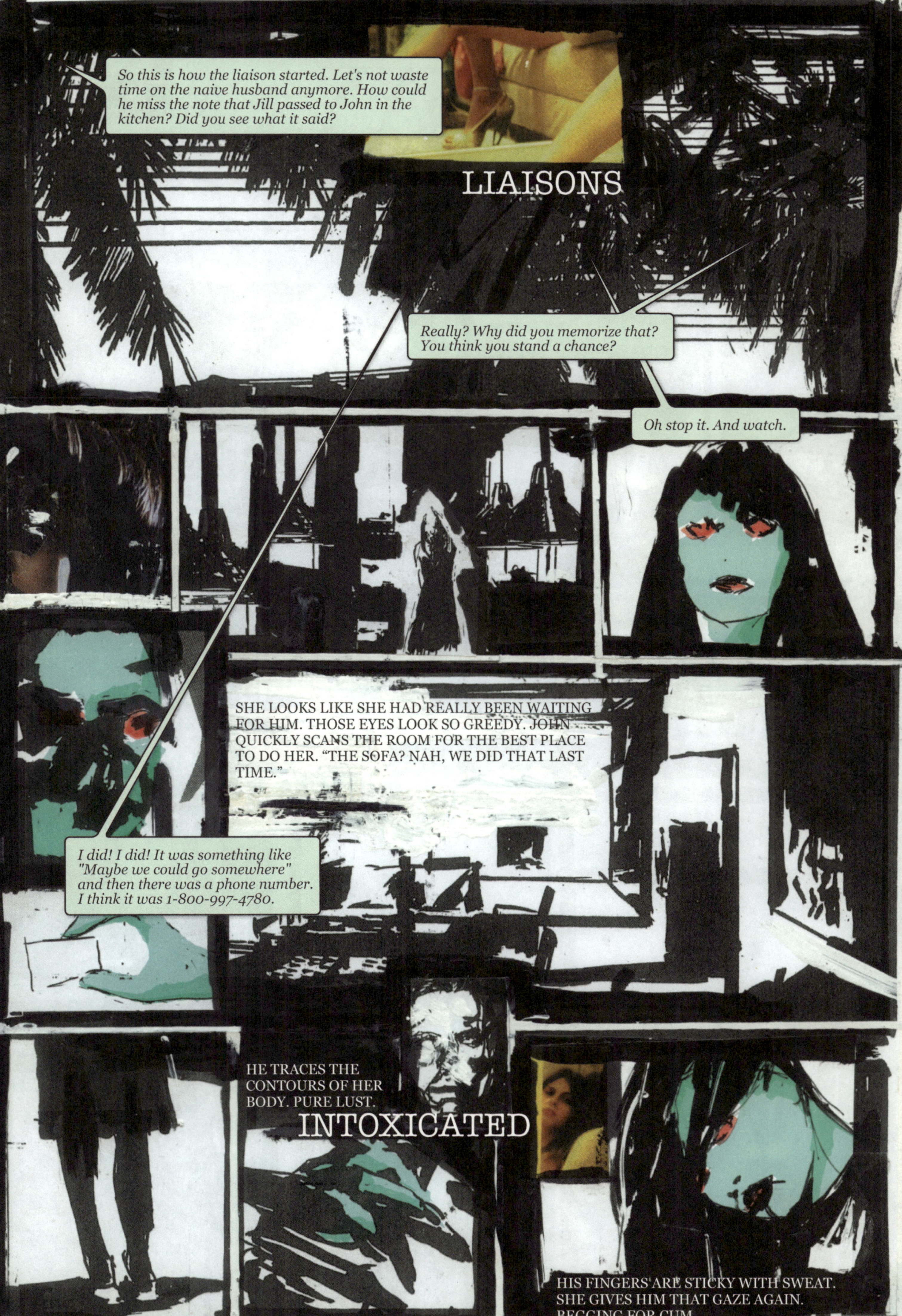
So this is how the liaison started. Let's not waste time on the naive husband anymore. How could he miss the note that Jill passed to John in the kitchen? Did you see what it said?

LIAISONS

Really? Why did you memorize that? You think you stand a chance?

Oh stop it. And watch.

SHE LOOKS LIKE SHE HAD REALLY BEEN WAITING FOR HIM. THOSE EYES LOOK SO GREEDY. JOHN QUICKLY SCANS THE ROOM FOR THE BEST PLACE TO DO HER. "THE SOFA? NAH, WE DID THAT LAST TIME."

I did! I did! It was something like "Maybe we could go somewhere" and then there was a phone number. I think it was 1-800-997-4780.

HE TRACES THE CONTOURS OF HER BODY. PURE LUST.

INTOXICATED

HIS FINGERS ARE STICKY WITH SWEAT. SHE GIVES HIM THAT GAZE AGAIN. BEGGING FOR CUM.

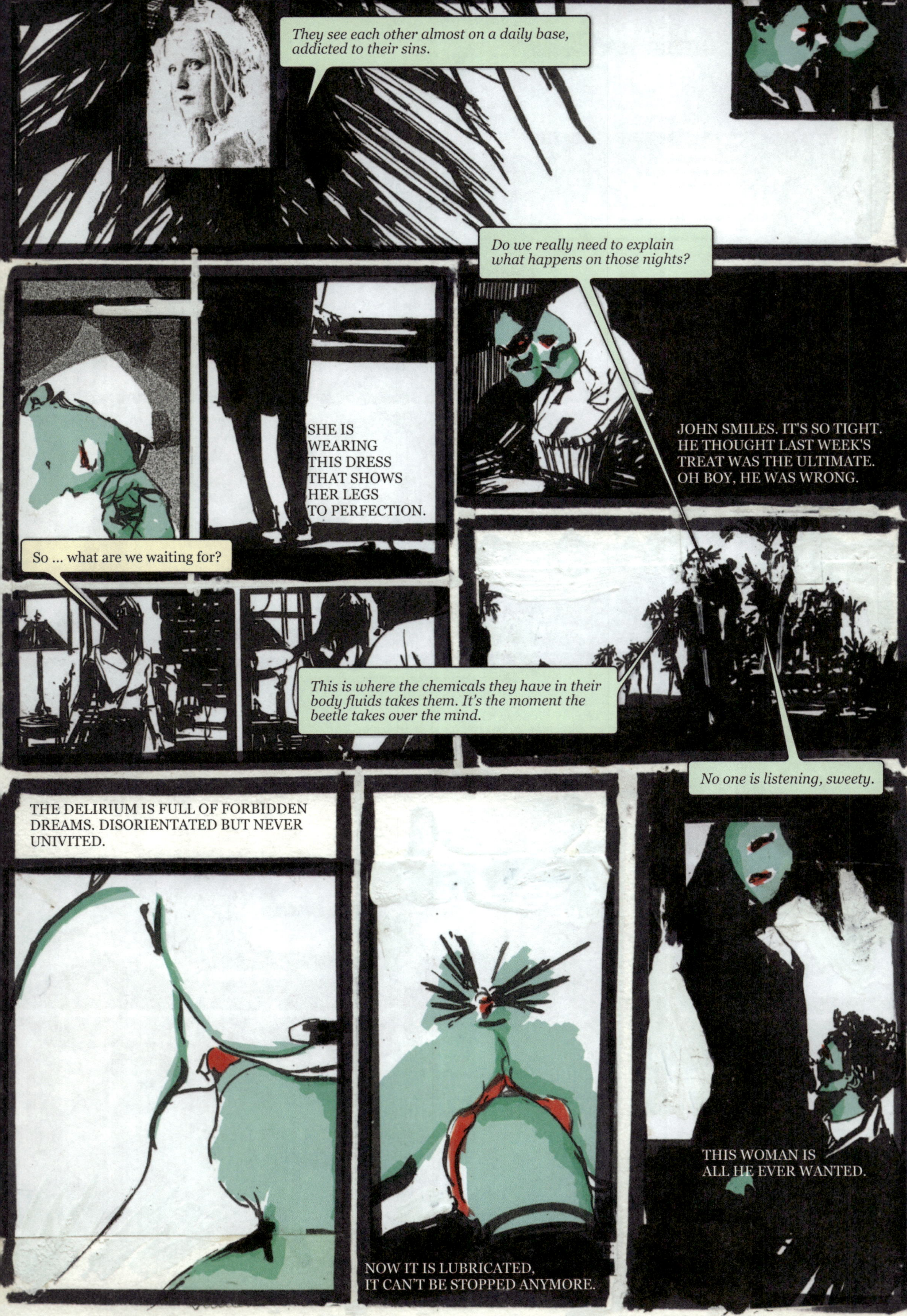

They see each other almost on a daily base, addicted to their sins.
Do we really need to explain what happens on those nights?
SHE IS WEARING THIS DRESS THAT SHOWS HER LEGS TO PERFECTION.
JOHN SMILES. IT'S SO TIGHT. HE THOUGHT LAST WEEK'S TREAT WAS THE ULTIMATE. OH BOY, HE WAS WRONG.
So ... what are we waiting for?
This is where the chemicals they have in their body fluids takes them. It's the moment the beetle takes over the mind.
No one is listening, sweety.
THE DELIRIUM IS FULL OF FORBIDDEN DREAMS. DISORIENTATED BUT NEVER UNIVITED.
THIS WOMAN IS ALL HE EVER WANTED.
NOW IT IS LUBRICATED, IT CAN'T BE STOPPED ANYMORE.

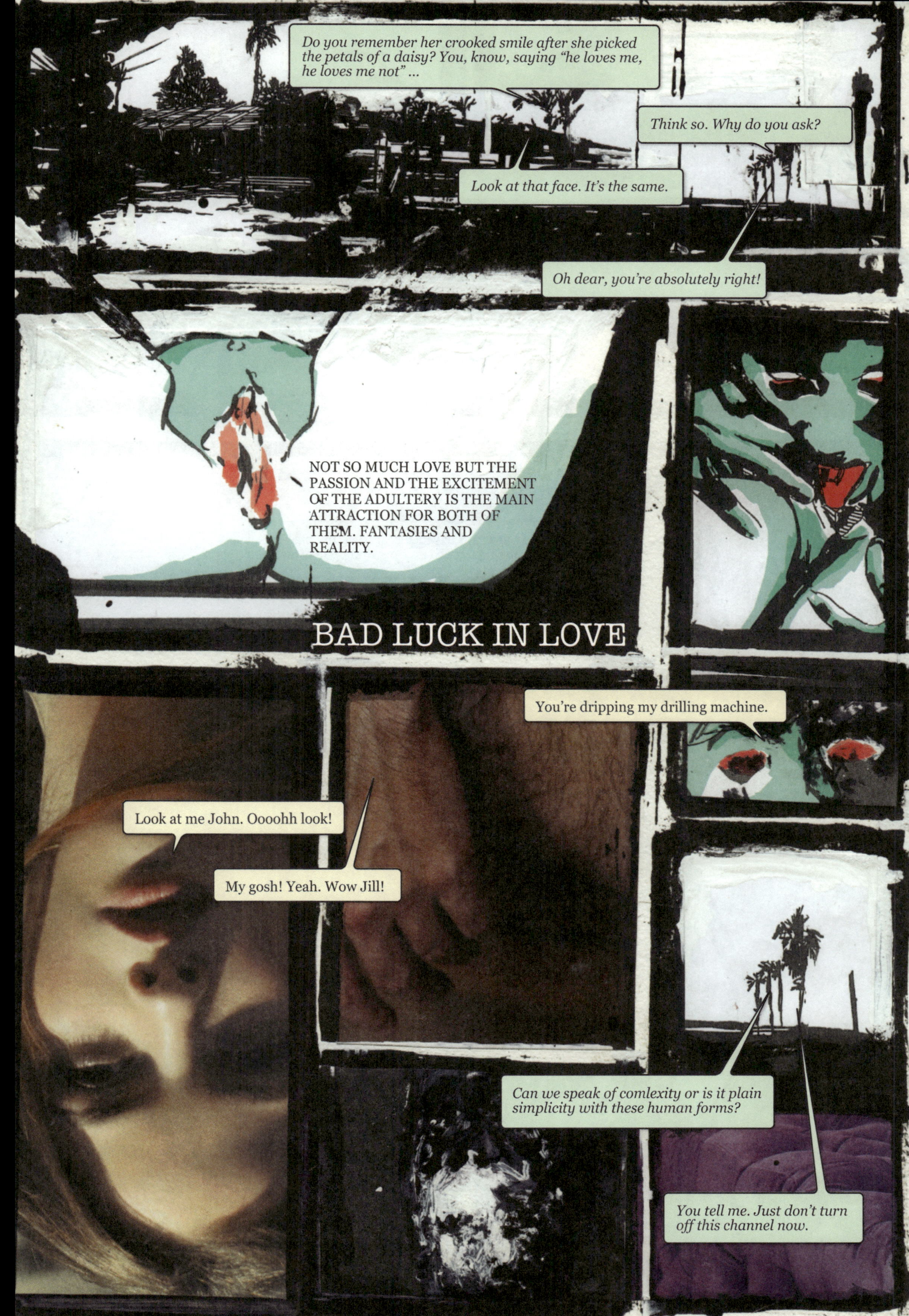

Do you remember her crooked smile after she picked the petals of a daisy? You, know, saying "he loves me, he loves me not" ...
Think so. Why do you ask?
Look at that face. It's the same.
Oh dear, you're absolutely right!
NOT SO MUCH LOVE BUT THE PASSION AND THE EXCITEMENT OF THE ADULTERY IS THE MAIN ATTRACTION FOR BOTH OF THEM. FANTASIES AND REALITY.
BAD LUCK IN LOVE
You're dripping my drilling machine.
Look at me John. Oooohh look!
My gosh! Yeah. Wow Jill!
Can we speak of comlexity or is it plain simplicity with these human forms?
You tell me. Just don't turn off this channel now.

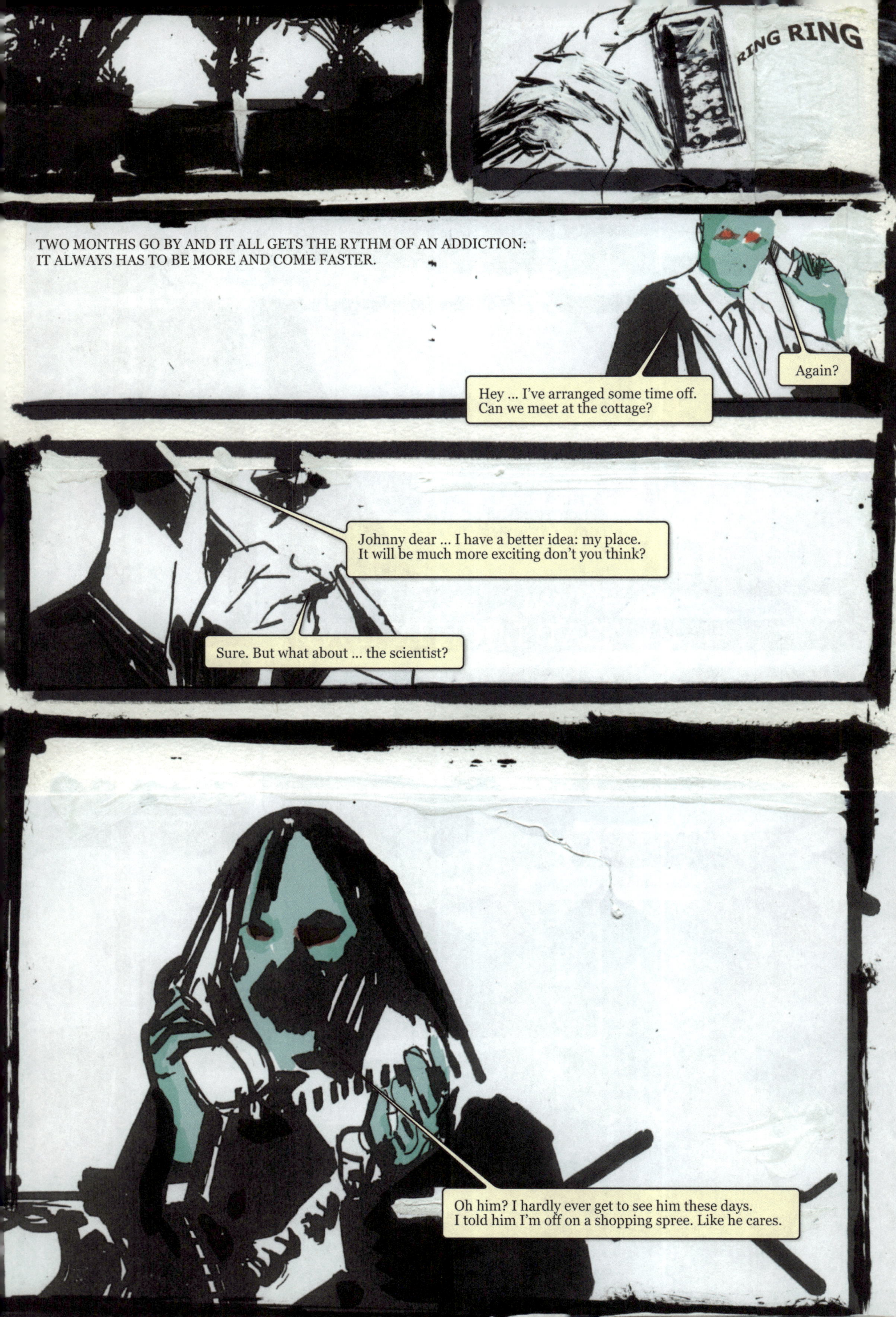

RING RING
TWO MONTHS GO BY AND IT ALL GETS THE RYTHM OF AN ADDICTION:
IT ALWAYS HAS TO BE MORE AND COME FASTER.
Again?
Hey ... I've arranged some time off.
Can we meet at the cottage?
Johnny dear ... I have a better idea: my place.
It will be much more exciting don't you think?
Sure. But what about ... the scientist?
Oh him? I hardly ever get to see him these days.
I told him I'm off on a shopping spree. Like he cares.

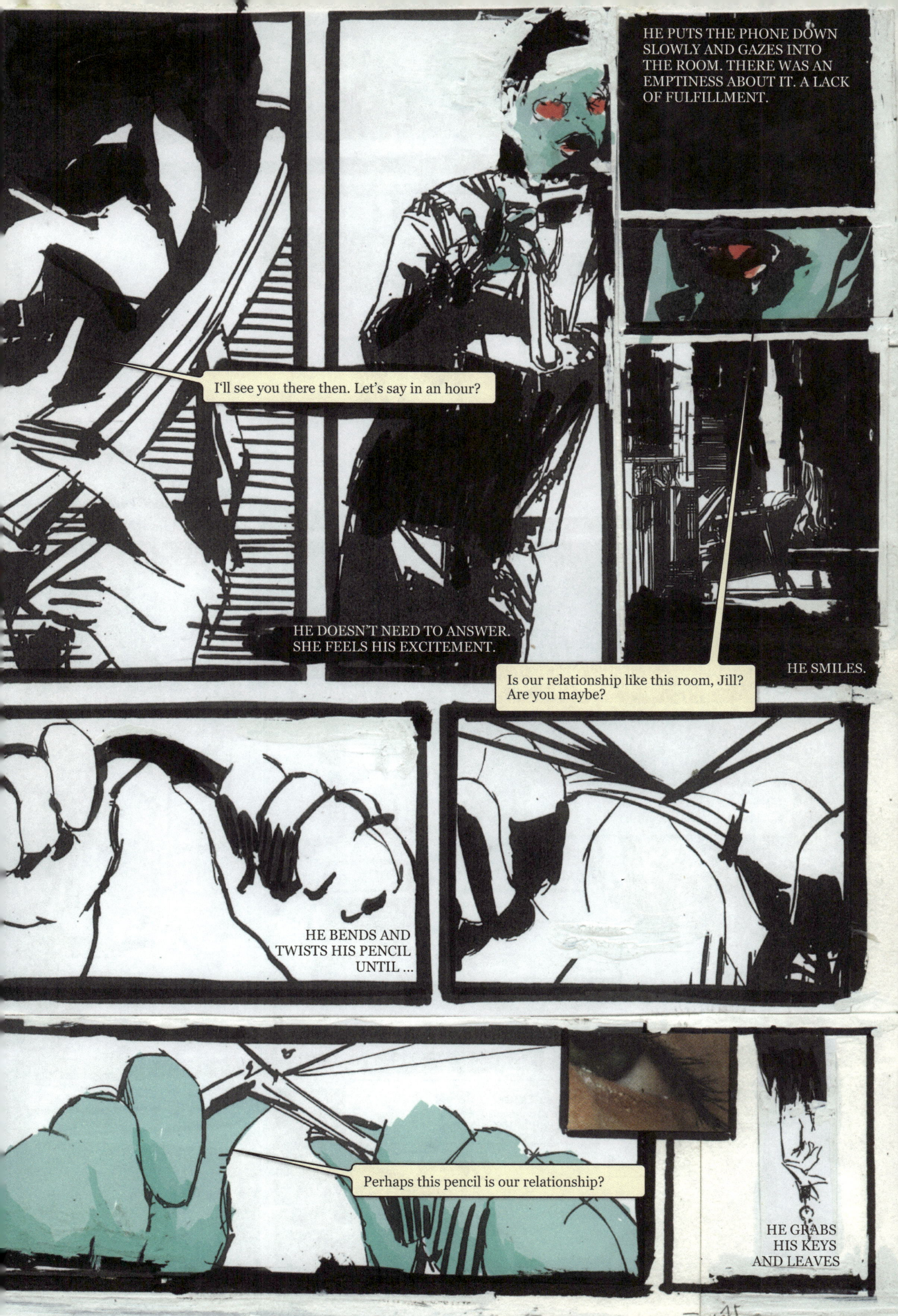

HE PUTS THE PHONE DOWN SLOWLY AND GAZES INTO THE ROOM. THERE WAS AN EMPTINESS ABOUT IT. A LACK OF FULFILLMENT.
I'll see you there then. Let's say in an hour?
HE DOESN'T NEED TO ANSWER. SHE FEELS HIS EXCITEMENT.
Is our relationship like this room, Jill? Are you maybe?
HE SMILES.
HE BENDS AND TWISTS HIS PENCIL UNTIL …
Perhaps this pencil is our relationship?
HE GRABS HIS KEYS AND LEAVES

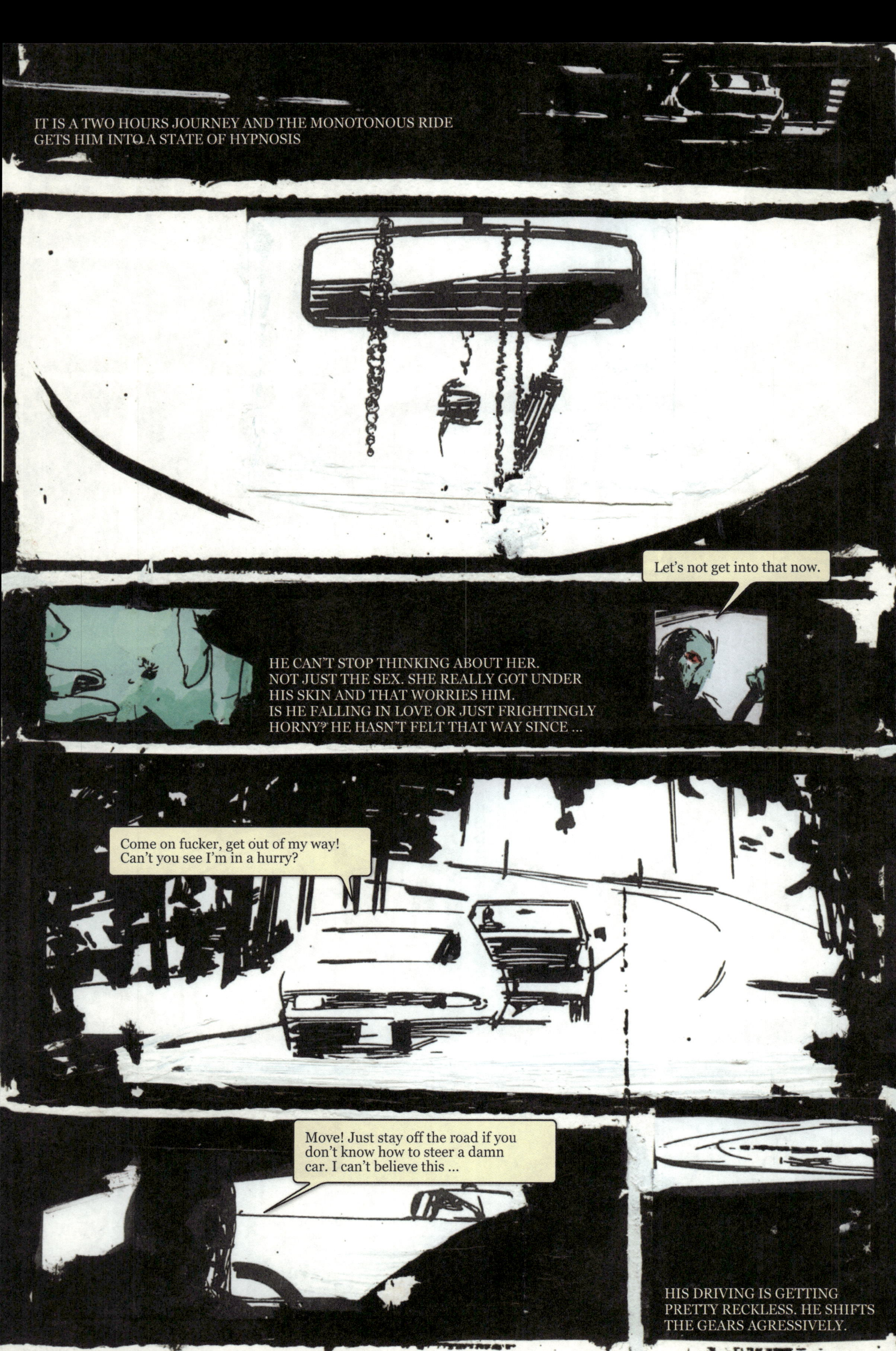

IT IS A TWO HOURS JOURNEY AND THE MONOTONOUS RIDE
GETS HIM INTO A STATE OF HYPNOSIS
Let's not get into that now.
HE CAN'T STOP THINKING ABOUT HER.
NOT JUST THE SEX. SHE REALLY GOT UNDER
HIS SKIN AND THAT WORRIES HIM.
IS HE FALLING IN LOVE OR JUST FRIGHTINGLY
HORNY? HE HASN'T FELT THAT WAY SINCE …
Come on fucker, get out of my way!
Can't you see I'm in a hurry?
Move! Just stay off the road if you
don't know how to steer a damn
car. I can't believe this …
HIS DRIVING IS GETTING
PRETTY RECKLESS. HE SHIFTS
THE GEARS AGRESSIVELY.

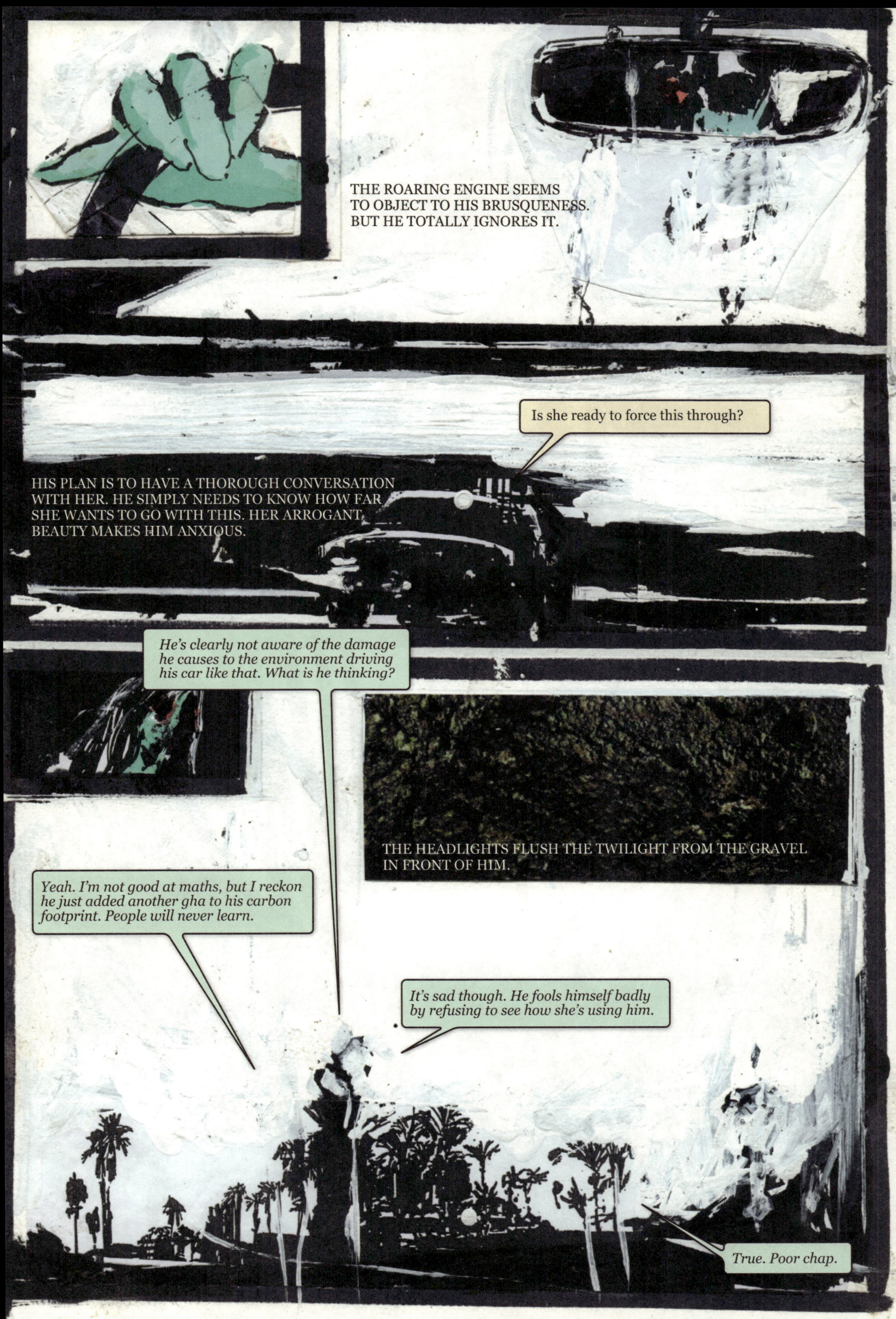

THE ROARING ENGINE SEEMS TO OBJECT TO HIS BRUSQUENESS. BUT HE TOTALLY IGNORES IT.
Is she ready to force this through?
HIS PLAN IS TO HAVE A THOROUGH CONVERSATION WITH HER. HE SIMPLY NEEDS TO KNOW HOW FAR SHE WANTS TO GO WITH THIS. HER ARROGANT BEAUTY MAKES HIM ANXIOUS.
He's clearly not aware of the damage he causes to the environment driving his car like that. What is he thinking?
THE HEADLIGHTS FLUSH THE TWILIGHT FROM THE GRAVEL IN FRONT OF HIM.
Yeah. I'm not good at maths, but I reckon he just added another gha to his carbon footprint. People will never learn.
It's sad though. He fools himself badly by refusing to see how she's using him.
True. Poor chap.

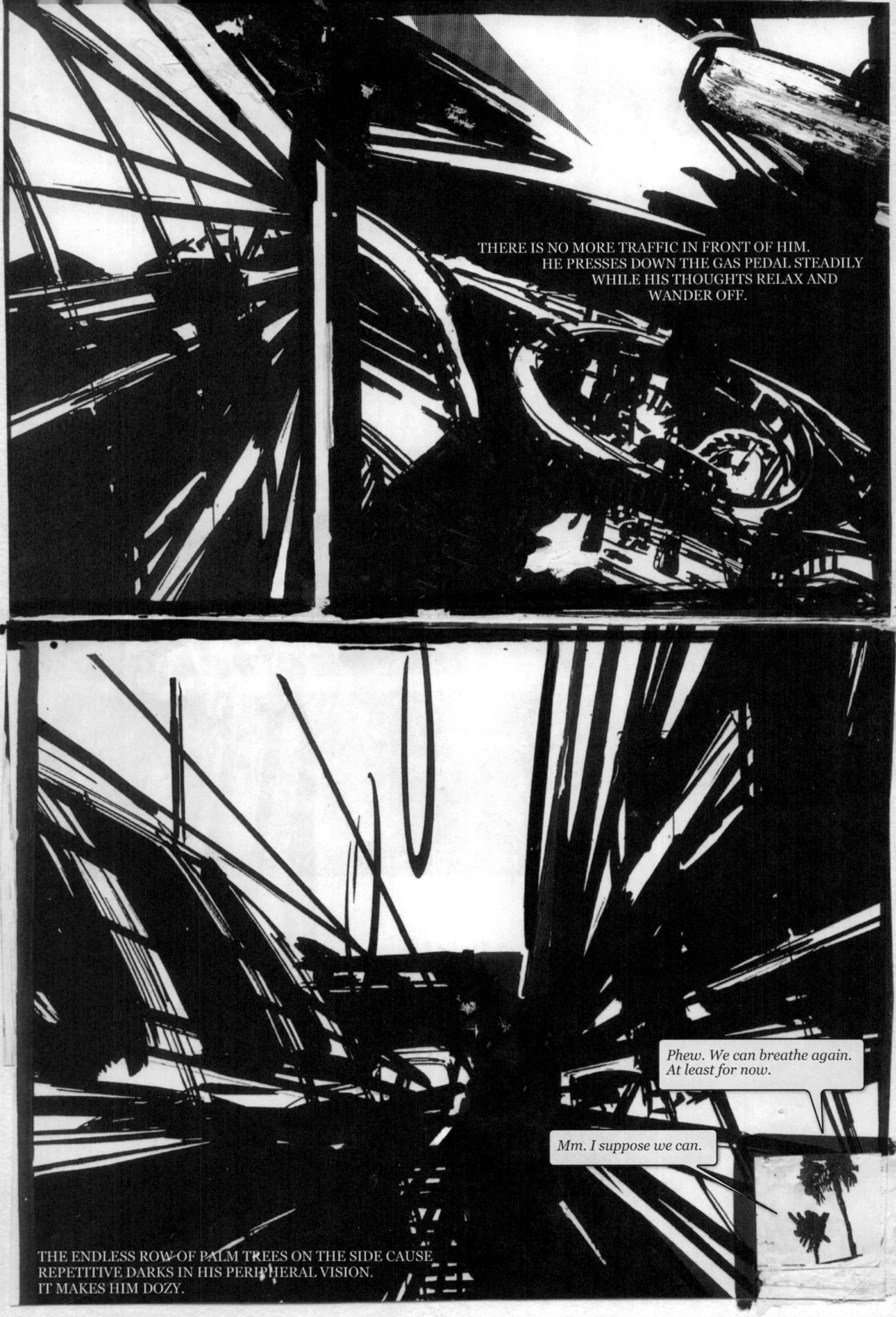

THERE IS NO MORE TRAFFIC IN FRONT OF HIM. HE PRESSES DOWN THE GAS PEDAL STEADILY WHILE HIS THOUGHTS RELAX AND WANDER OFF.
Phew. We can breathe again. At least for now.
Mm. I suppose we can.
THE ENDLESS ROW OF PALM TREES ON THE SIDE CAUSE REPETITIVE DARKS IN HIS PERIPHERAL VISION. IT MAKES HIM DOZY.

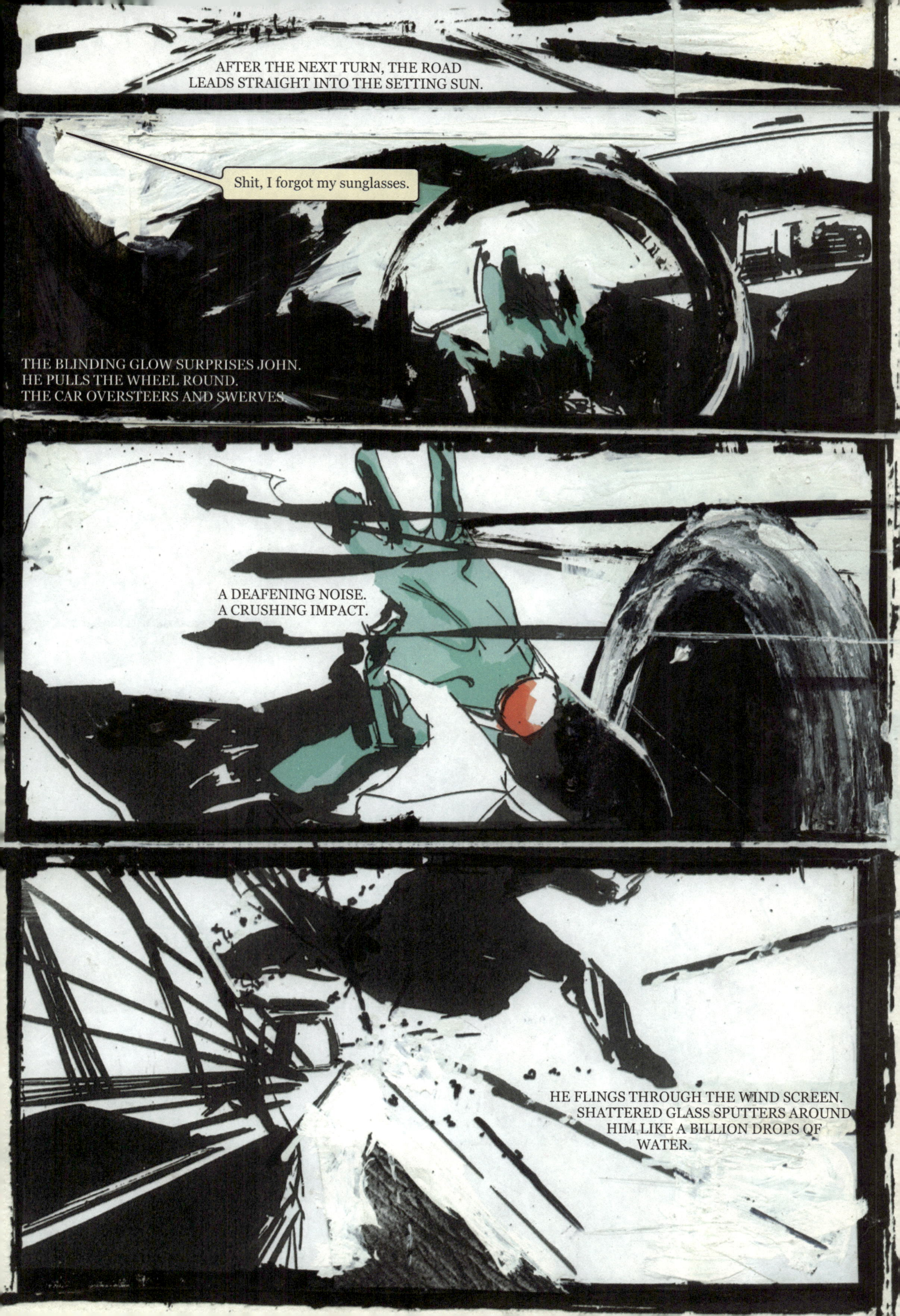

AFTER THE NEXT TURN, THE ROAD LEADS STRAIGHT INTO THE SETTING SUN.
Shit, I forgot my sunglasses.
THE BLINDING GLOW SURPRISES JOHN. HE PULLS THE WHEEL ROUND. THE CAR OVERSTEERS AND SWERVES
A DEAFENING NOISE. A CRUSHING IMPACT.
HE FLINGS THROUGH THE WIND SCREEN. SHATTERED GLASS SPUTTERS AROUND HIM LIKE A BILLION DROPS OF WATER.

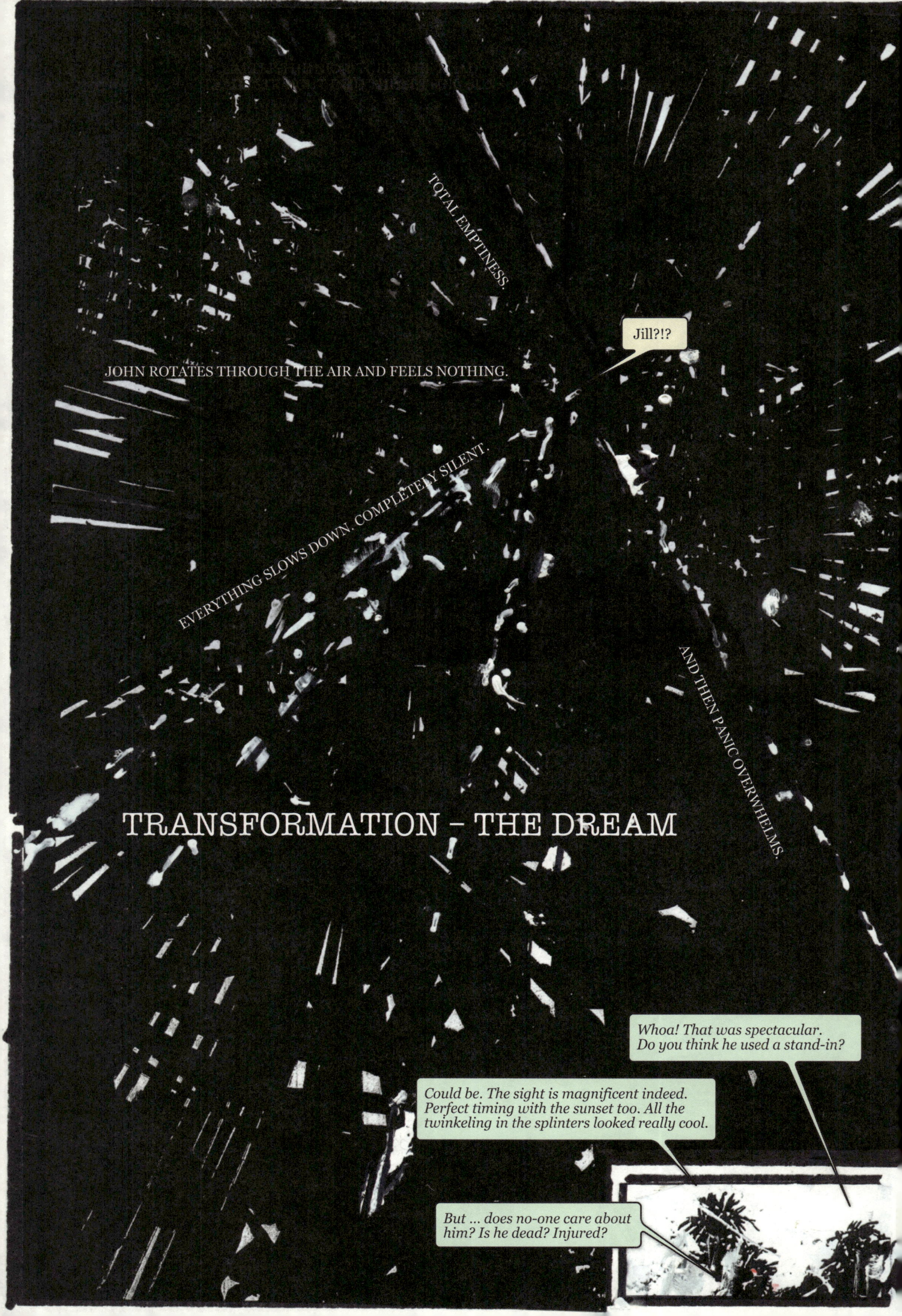

TOTAL EMPTINESS.

Jill?!?

JOHN ROTATES THROUGH THE AIR AND FEELS NOTHING.

EVERYTHING SLOWS DOWN. COMPLETELY SILENT.

AND THEN PANIC OVERWHELMS.

TRANSFORMATION – THE DREAM

Whoa! That was spectacular.
Do you think he used a stand-in?

Could be. The sight is magnificent indeed.
Perfect timing with the sunset too. All the
twinkeling in the splinters looked really cool.

But ... does no-one care about
him? Is he dead? Injured?

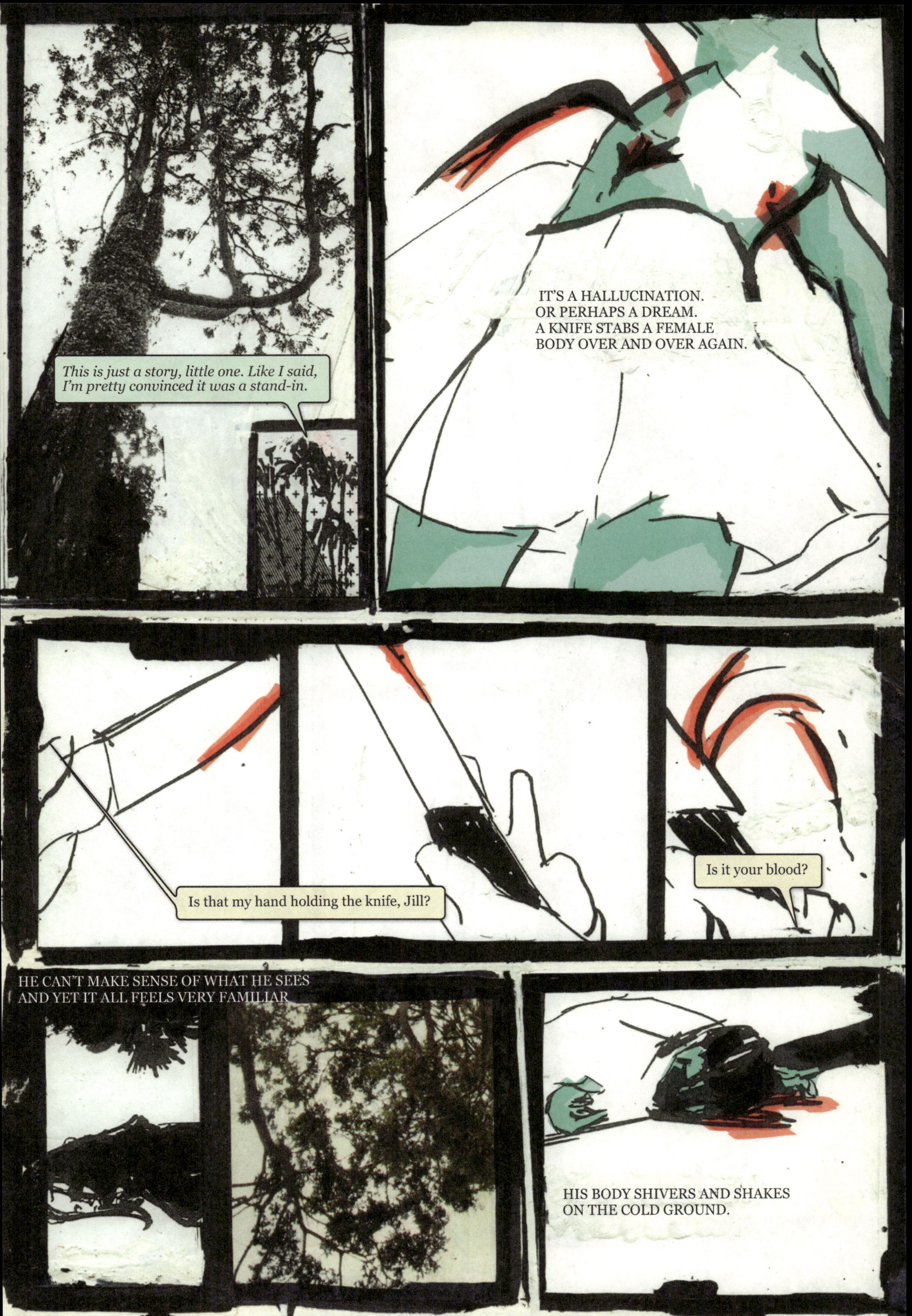
This is just a story, little one. Like I said, I'm pretty convinced it was a stand-in.
IT'S A HALLUCINATION. OR PERHAPS A DREAM. A KNIFE STABS A FEMALE BODY OVER AND OVER AGAIN.
Is that my hand holding the knife, Jill?
Is it your blood?
HE CAN'T MAKE SENSE OF WHAT HE SEES AND YET IT ALL FEELS VERY FAMILIAR
HIS BODY SHIVERS AND SHAKES ON THE COLD GROUND.

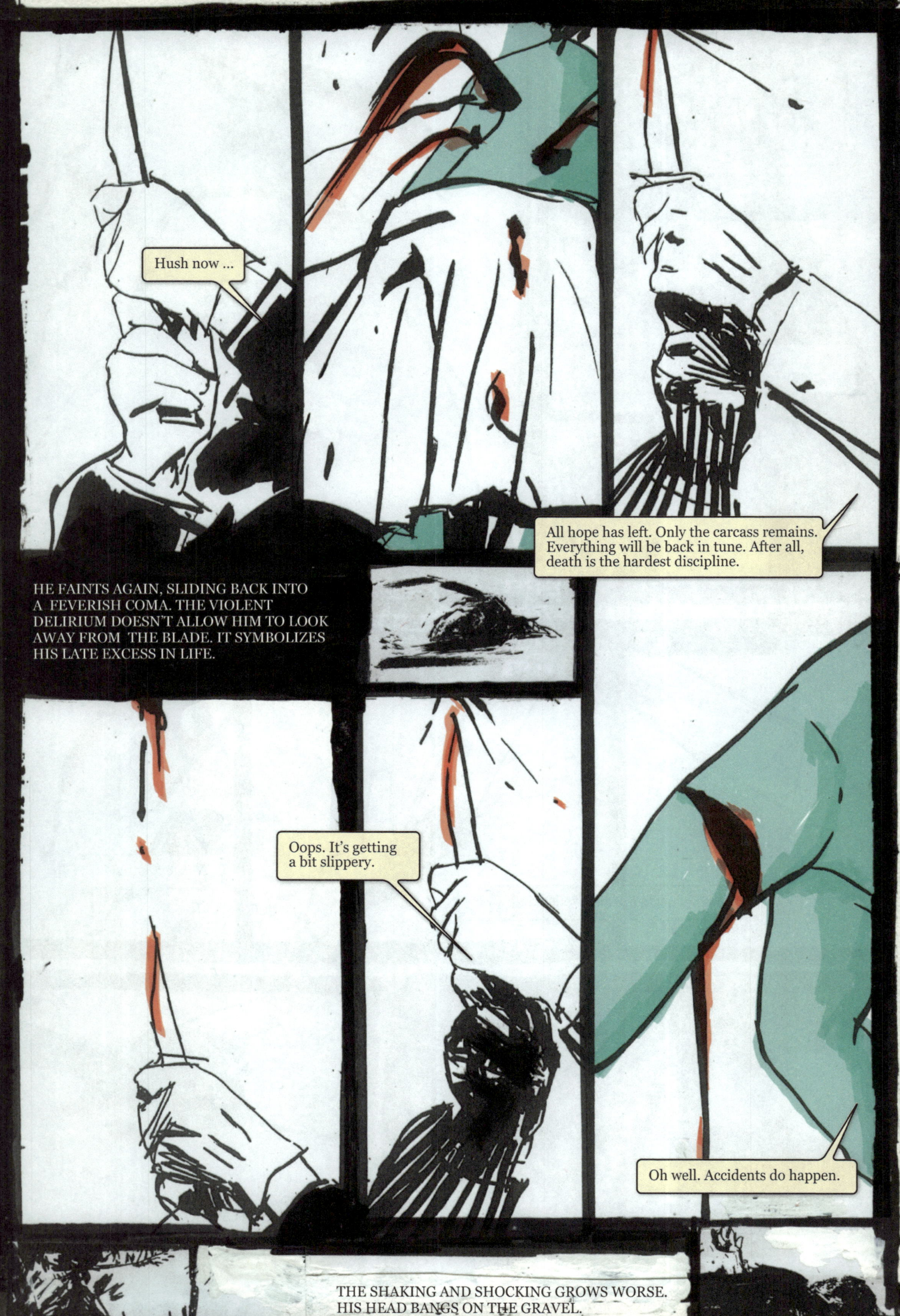

Hush now ...
All hope has left. Only the carcass remains. Everything will be back in tune. After all, death is the hardest discipline.
HE FAINTS AGAIN, SLIDING BACK INTO A FEVERISH COMA. THE VIOLENT DELIRIUM DOESN'T ALLOW HIM TO LOOK AWAY FROM THE BLADE. IT SYMBOLIZES HIS LATE EXCESS IN LIFE.
Oops. It's getting a bit slippery.
Oh well. Accidents do happen.
THE SHAKING AND SHOCKING GROWS WORSE. HIS HEAD BANGS ON THE GRAVEL.

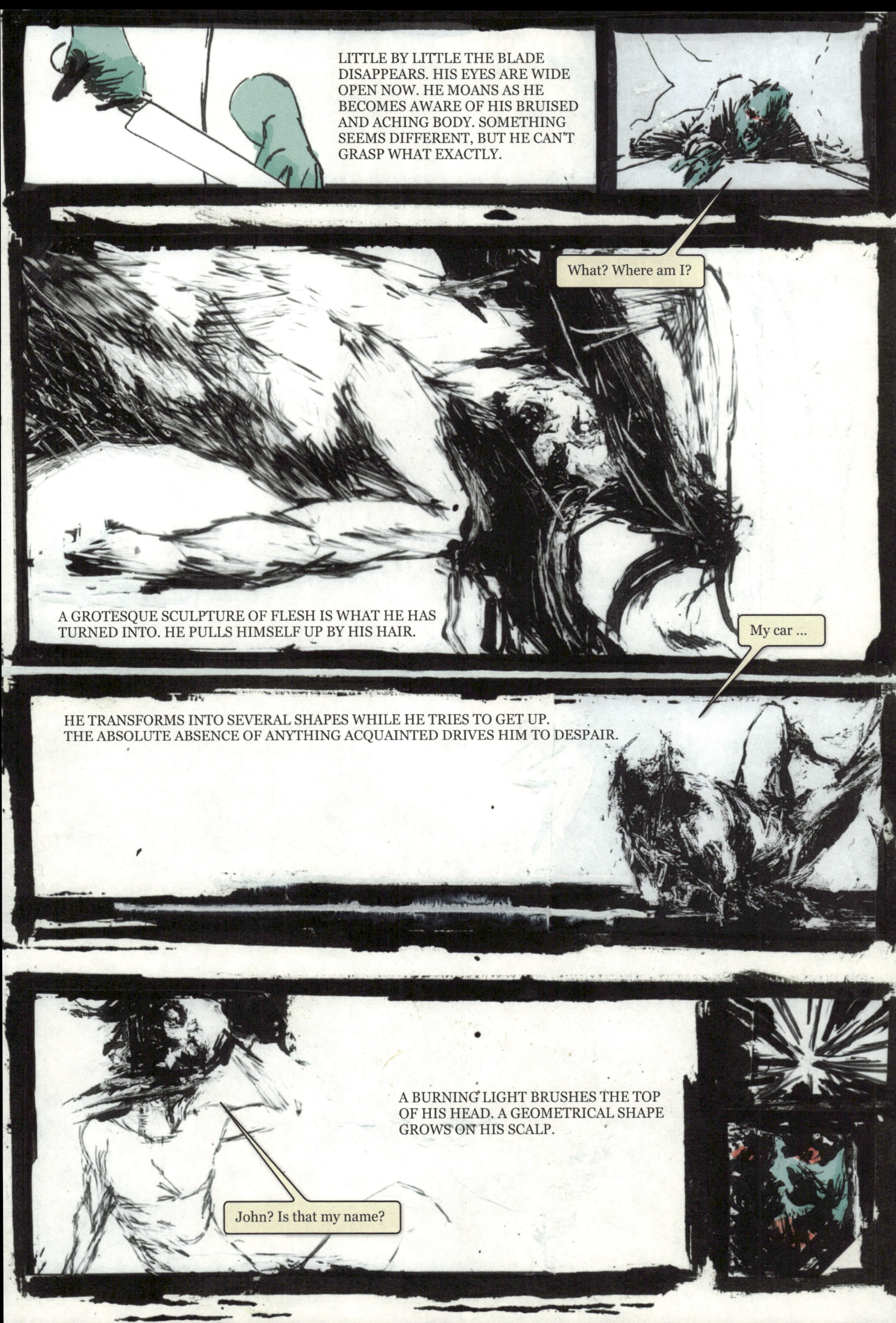

LITTLE BY LITTLE THE BLADE DISAPPEARS. HIS EYES ARE WIDE OPEN NOW. HE MOANS AS HE BECOMES AWARE OF HIS BRUISED AND ACHING BODY. SOMETHING SEEMS DIFFERENT, BUT HE CAN'T GRASP WHAT EXACTLY.
What? Where am I?
A GROTESQUE SCULPTURE OF FLESH IS WHAT HE HAS TURNED INTO. HE PULLS HIMSELF UP BY HIS HAIR.
My car ...
HE TRANSFORMS INTO SEVERAL SHAPES WHILE HE TRIES TO GET UP. THE ABSOLUTE ABSENCE OF ANYTHING ACQUAINTED DRIVES HIM TO DESPAIR.
A BURNING LIGHT BRUSHES THE TOP OF HIS HEAD. A GEOMETRICAL SHAPE GROWS ON HIS SCALP.
John? Is that my name?

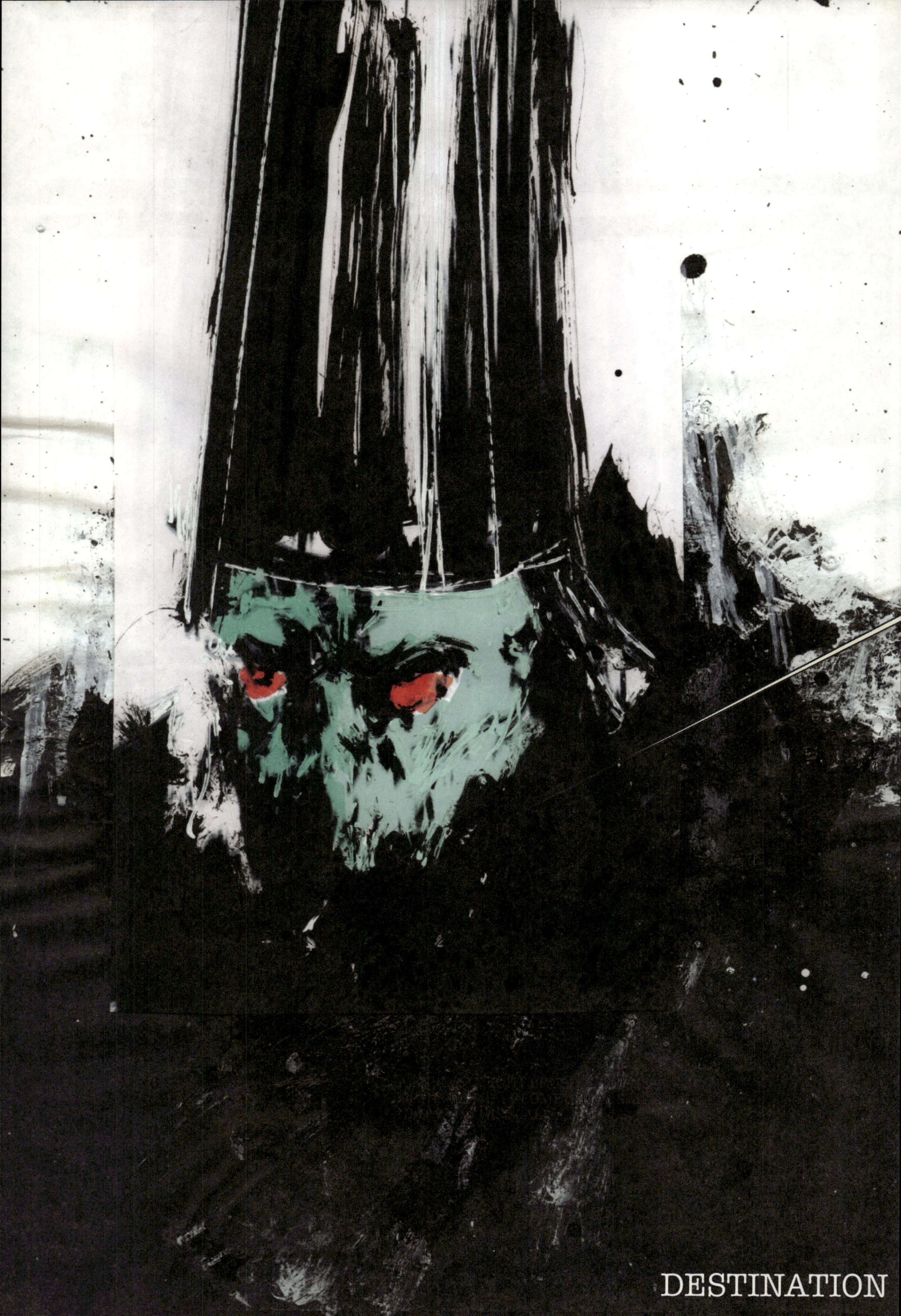
DESTINATION

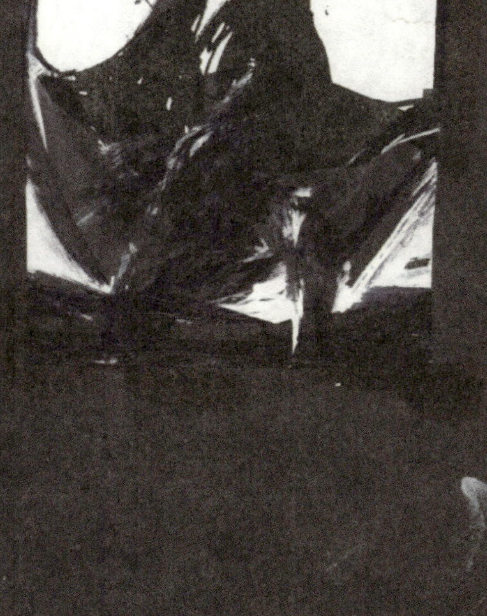
I know now.
For I am The Snowman!

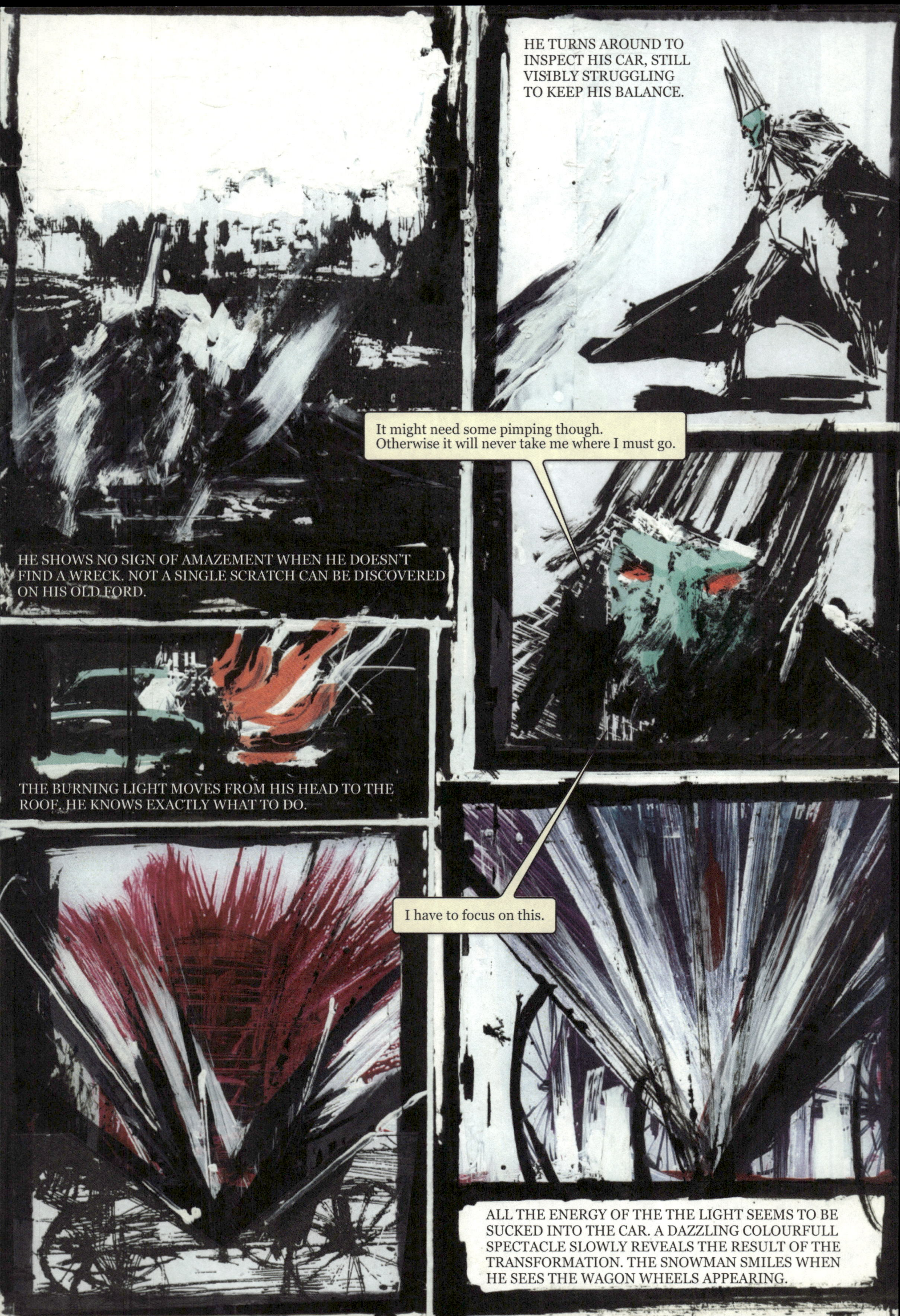
HE TURNS AROUND TO INSPECT HIS CAR, STILL VISIBLY STRUGGLING TO KEEP HIS BALANCE.
It might need some pimping though. Otherwise it will never take me where I must go.
HE SHOWS NO SIGN OF AMAZEMENT WHEN HE DOESN'T FIND A WRECK. NOT A SINGLE SCRATCH CAN BE DISCOVERED ON HIS OLD FORD.
THE BURNING LIGHT MOVES FROM HIS HEAD TO THE ROOF. HE KNOWS EXACTLY WHAT TO DO.
I have to focus on this.
ALL THE ENERGY OF THE THE LIGHT SEEMS TO BE SUCKED INTO THE CAR. A DAZZLING COLOURFULL SPECTACLE SLOWLY REVEALS THE RESULT OF THE TRANSFORMATION. THE SNOWMAN SMILES WHEN HE SEES THE WAGON WHEELS APPEARING.

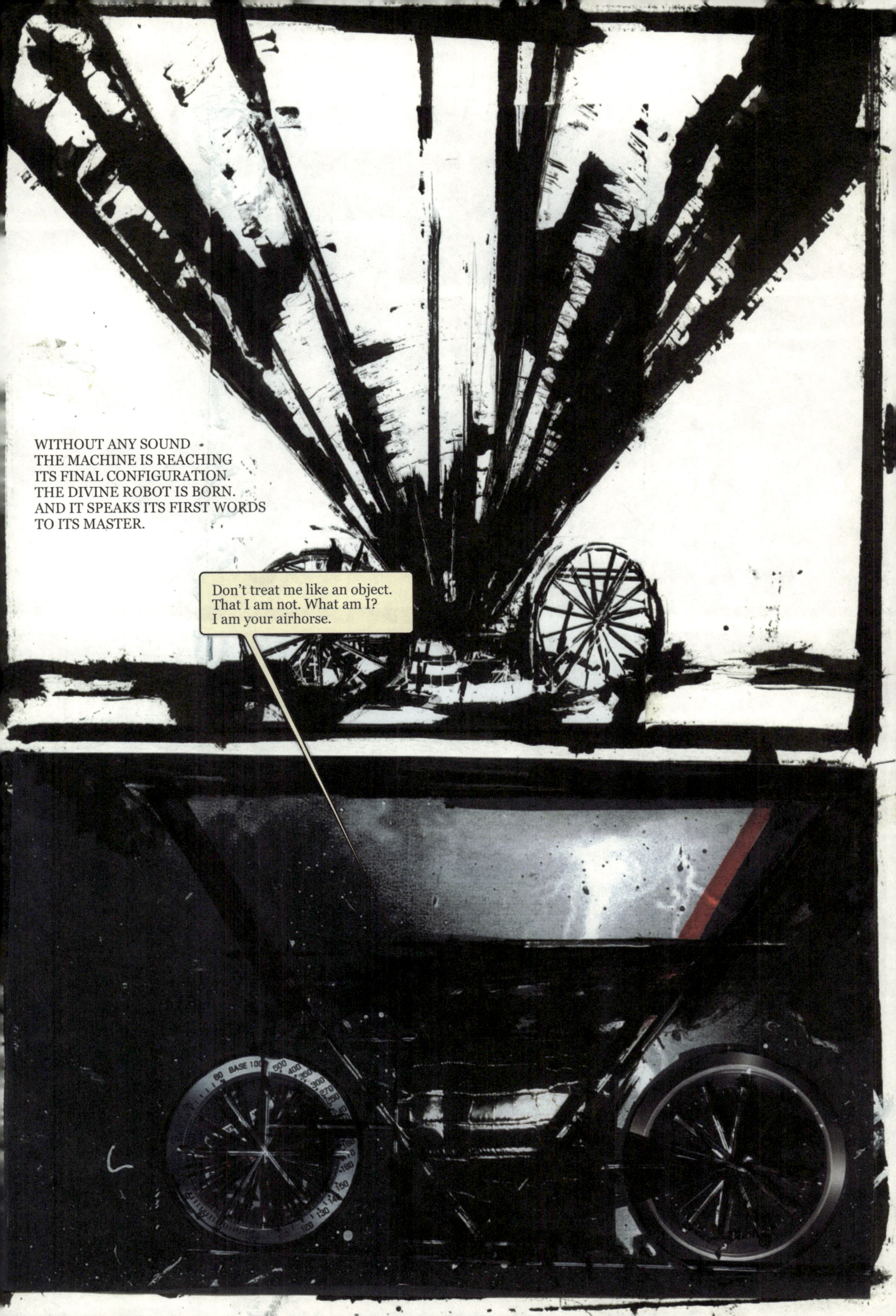

WITHOUT ANY SOUND
THE MACHINE IS REACHING
ITS FINAL CONFIGURATION.
THE DIVINE ROBOT IS BORN.
AND IT SPEAKS ITS FIRST WORDS
TO ITS MASTER.
Don't treat me like an object.
That I am not. What am I?
I am your airhorse.

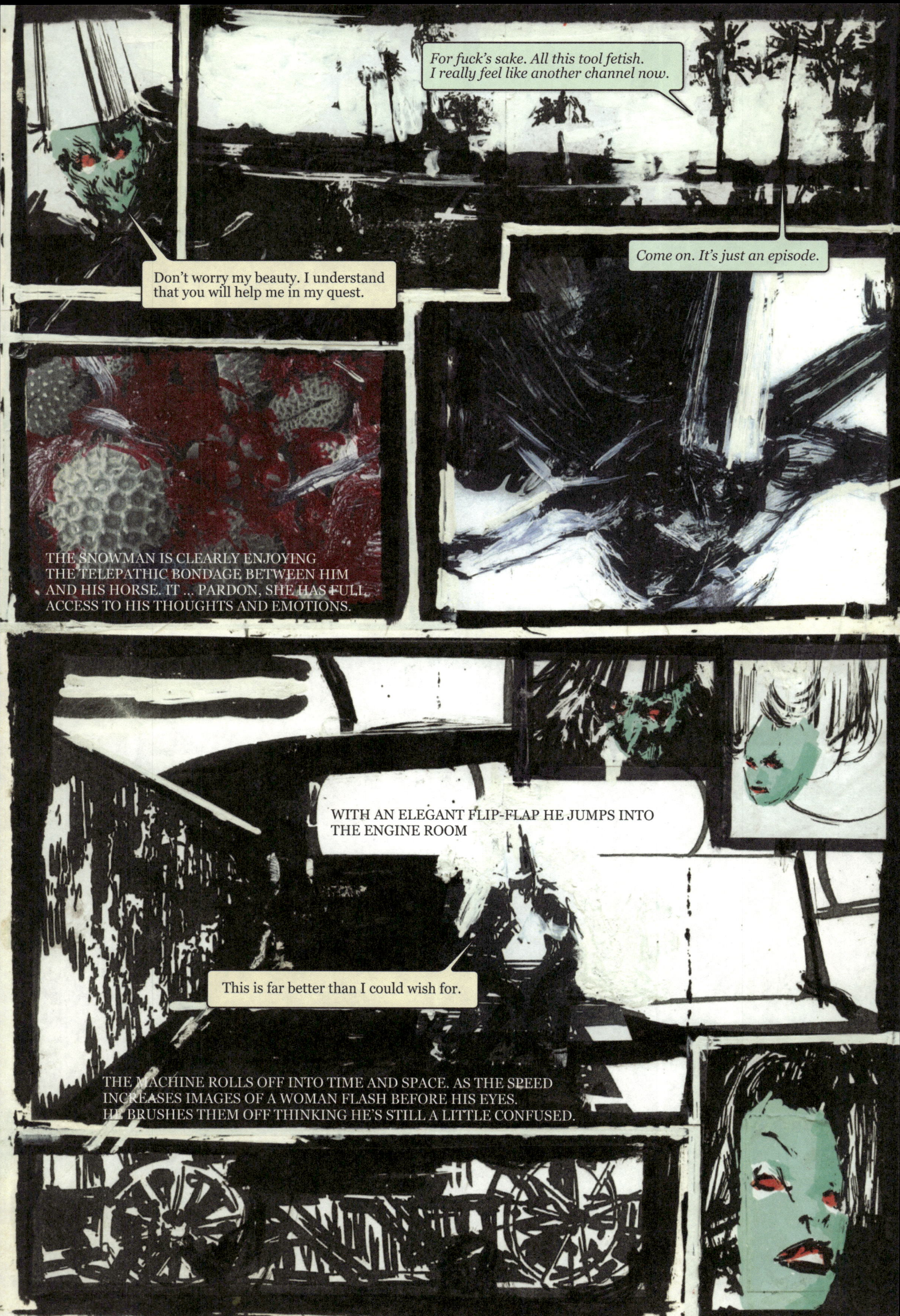

For fuck's sake. All this tool fetish. I really feel like another channel now.
Come on. It's just an episode.
Don't worry my beauty. I understand that you will help me in my quest.
THE SNOWMAN IS CLEARLY ENJOYING THE TELEPATHIC BONDAGE BETWEEN HIM AND HIS HORSE. IT ... PARDON, SHE HAS FULL ACCESS TO HIS THOUGHTS AND EMOTIONS.
WITH AN ELEGANT FLIP-FLAP HE JUMPS INTO THE ENGINE ROOM
This is far better than I could wish for.
THE MACHINE ROLLS OFF INTO TIME AND SPACE. AS THE SPEED INCREASES IMAGES OF A WOMAN FLASH BEFORE HIS EYES. HE BRUSHES THEM OFF THINKING HE'S STILL A LITTLE CONFUSED.

Part 2: The Squid

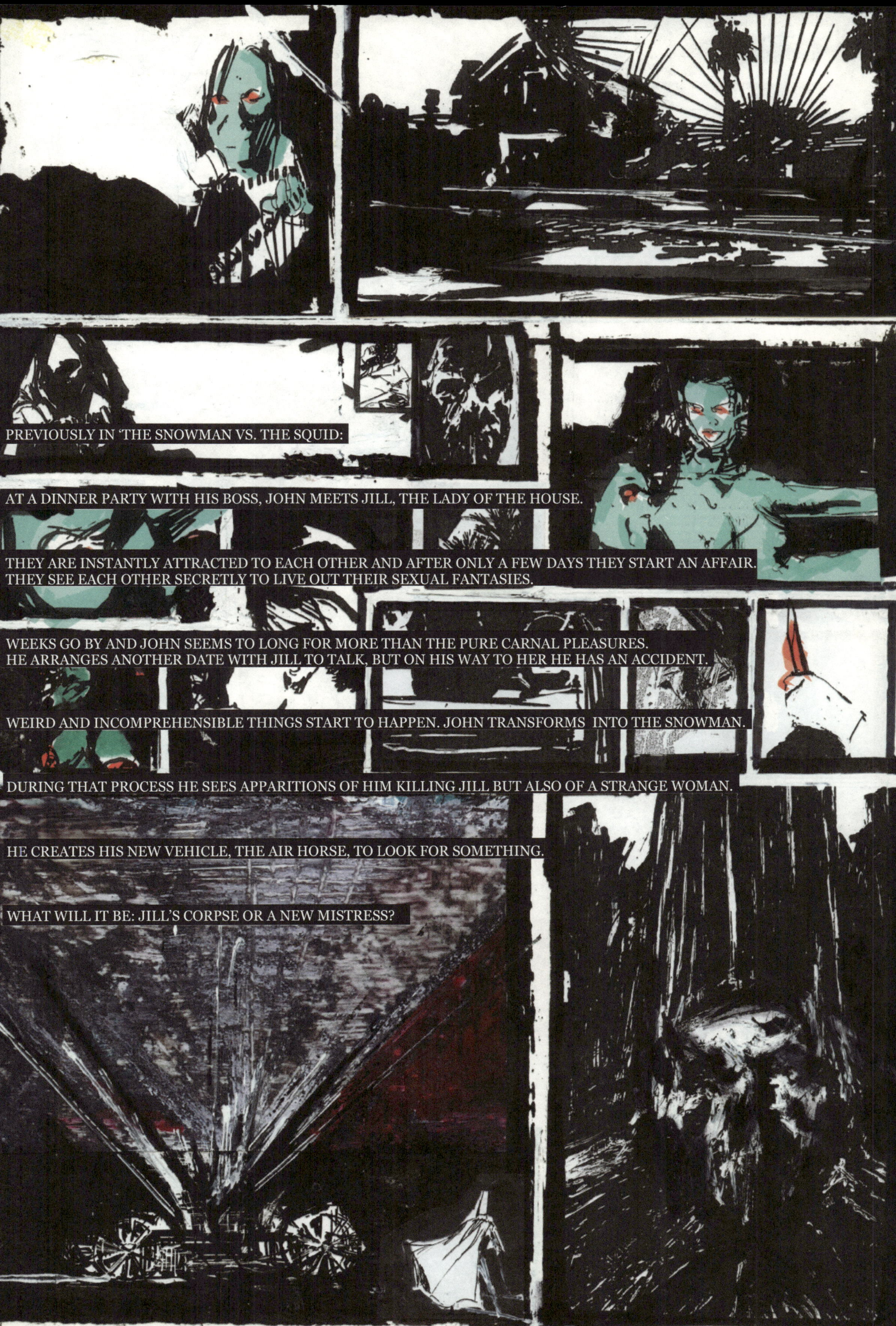

PREVIOUSLY IN 'THE SNOWMAN VS. THE SQUID:

AT A DINNER PARTY WITH HIS BOSS, JOHN MEETS JILL, THE LADY OF THE HOUSE.

THEY ARE INSTANTLY ATTRACTED TO EACH OTHER AND AFTER ONLY A FEW DAYS THEY START AN AFFAIR.
THEY SEE EACH OTHER SECRETLY TO LIVE OUT THEIR SEXUAL FANTASIES.

WEEKS GO BY AND JOHN SEEMS TO LONG FOR MORE THAN THE PURE CARNAL PLEASURES.
HE ARRANGES ANOTHER DATE WITH JILL TO TALK, BUT ON HIS WAY TO HER HE HAS AN ACCIDENT.

WEIRD AND INCOMPREHENSIBLE THINGS START TO HAPPEN. JOHN TRANSFORMS INTO THE SNOWMAN.

DURING THAT PROCESS HE SEES APPARITIONS OF HIM KILLING JILL BUT ALSO OF A STRANGE WOMAN.

HE CREATES HIS NEW VEHICLE, THE AIR HORSE, TO LOOK FOR SOMETHING.

WHAT WILL IT BE: JILL'S CORPSE OR A NEW MISTRESS?

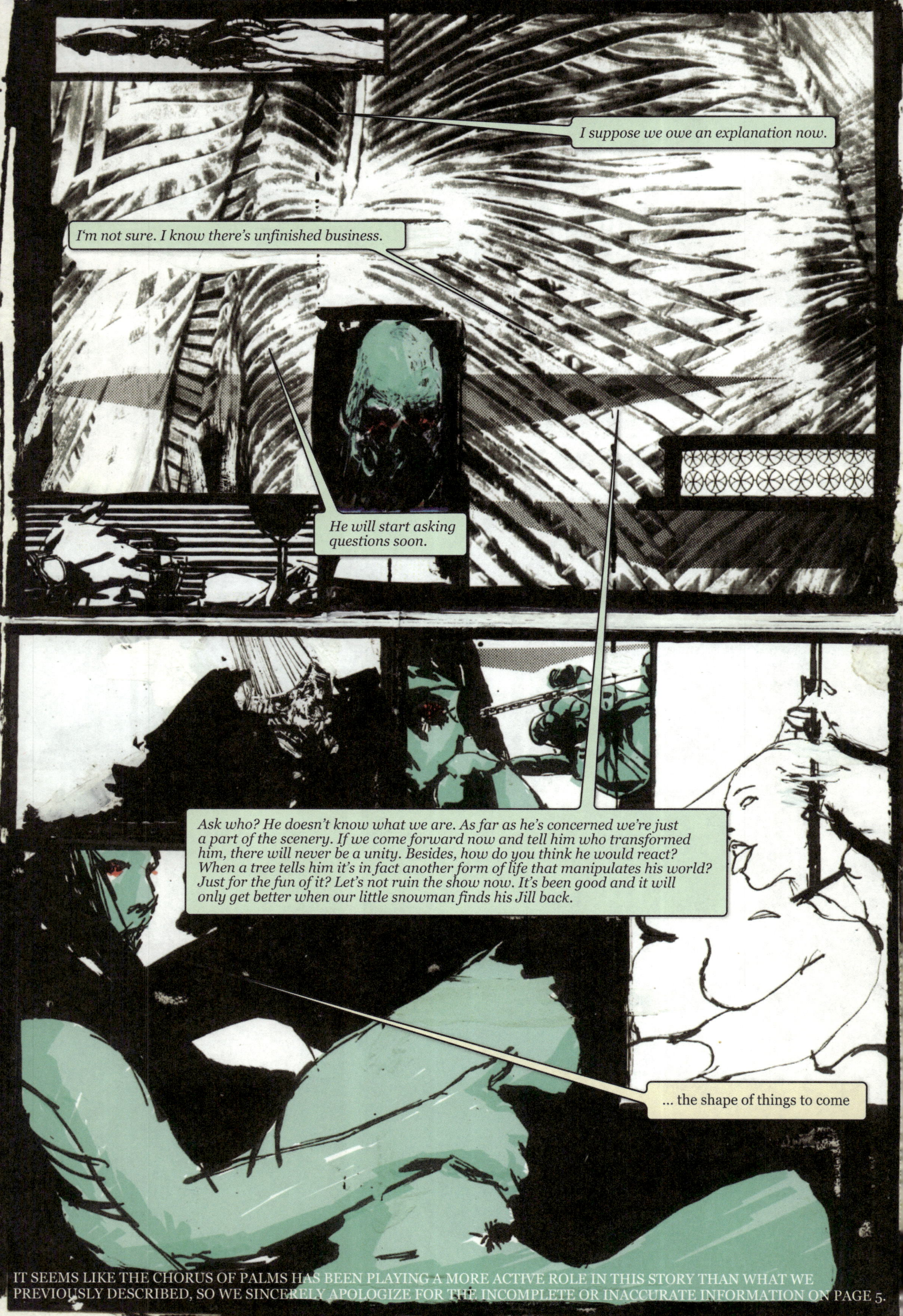

I suppose we owe an explanation now.
I'm not sure. I know there's unfinished business.
He will start asking questions soon.
Ask who? He doesn't know what we are. As far as he's concerned we're just a part of the scenery. If we come forward now and tell him who transformed him, there will never be a unity. Besides, how do you think he would react? When a tree tells him it's in fact another form of life that manipulates his world? Just for the fun of it? Let's not ruin the show now. It's been good and it will only get better when our little snowman finds his Jill back.
... the shape of things to come

THERE'S LIGHTNING

BUT NO RAIN WHATSOEVER. WE'RE AT SNOWMAN BASE.

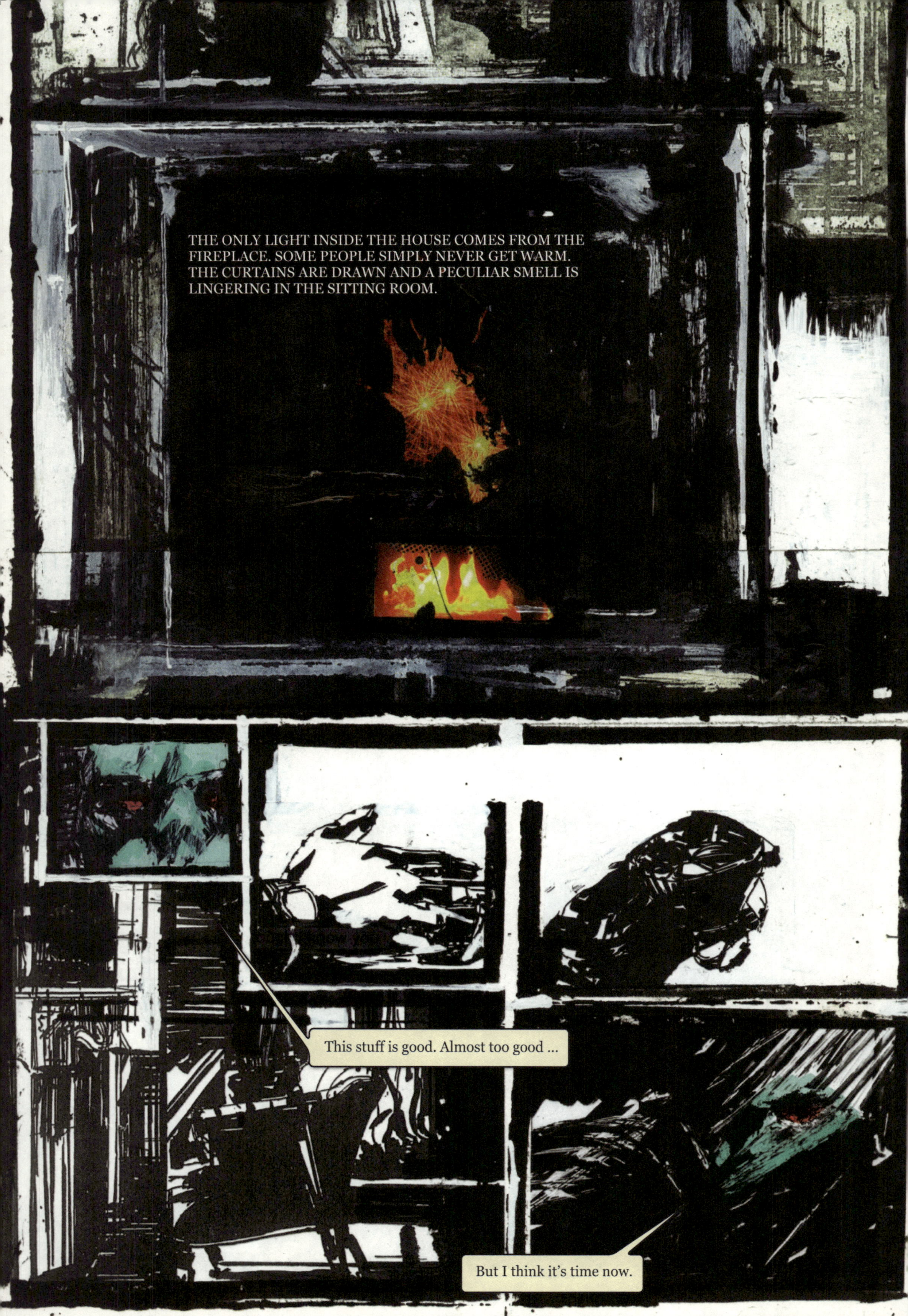

THE ONLY LIGHT INSIDE THE HOUSE COMES FROM THE FIREPLACE. SOME PEOPLE SIMPLY NEVER GET WARM. THE CURTAINS ARE DRAWN AND A PECULIAR SMELL IS LINGERING IN THE SITTING ROOM.
This stuff is good. Almost too good …
But I think it's time now.

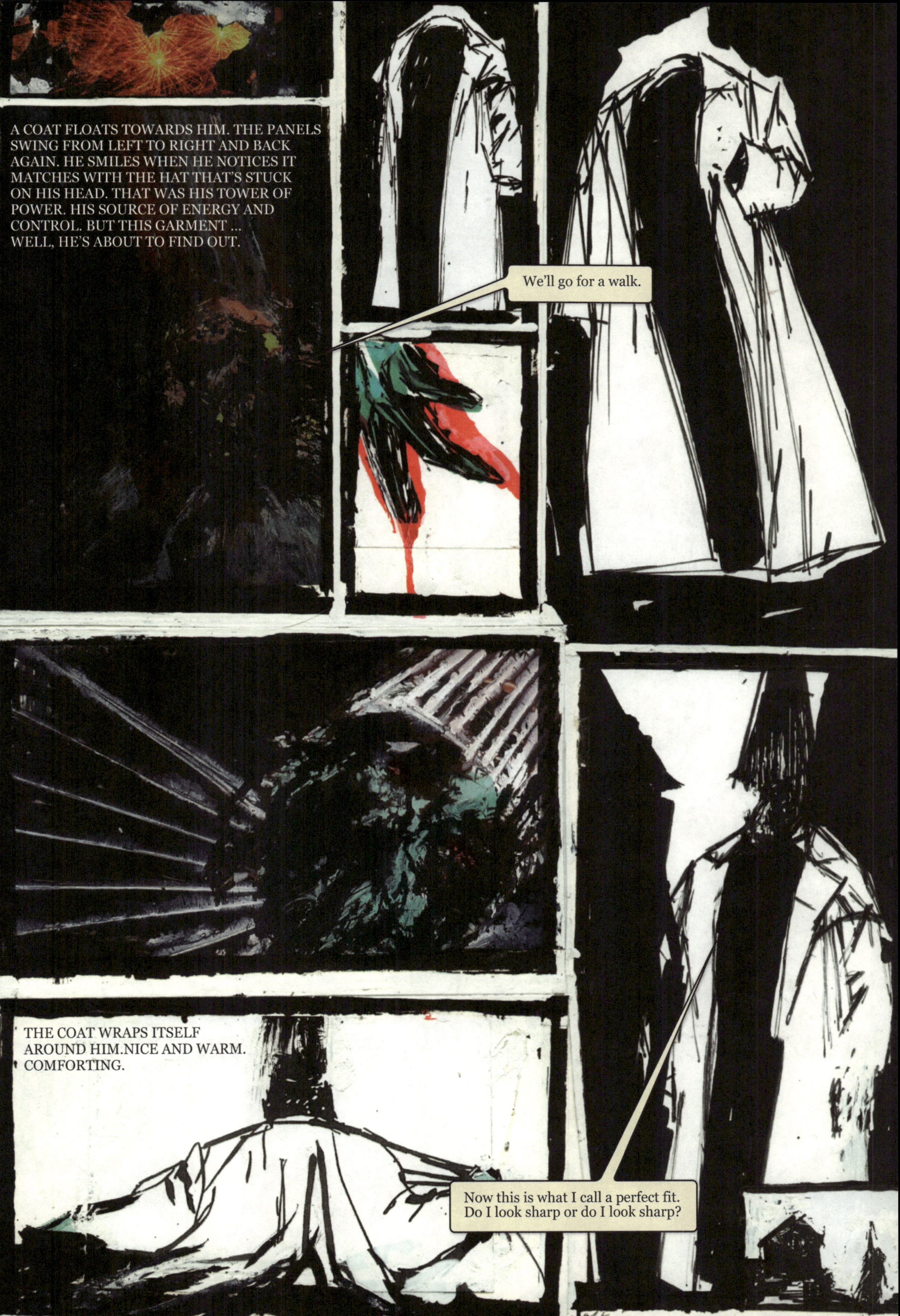

A COAT FLOATS TOWARDS HIM. THE PANELS SWING FROM LEFT TO RIGHT AND BACK AGAIN. HE SMILES WHEN HE NOTICES IT MATCHES WITH THE HAT THAT'S STUCK ON HIS HEAD. THAT WAS HIS TOWER OF POWER. HIS SOURCE OF ENERGY AND CONTROL. BUT THIS GARMENT … WELL, HE'S ABOUT TO FIND OUT.
We'll go for a walk.
THE COAT WRAPS ITSELF AROUND HIM. NICE AND WARM. COMFORTING.
Now this is what I call a perfect fit. Do I look sharp or do I look sharp?

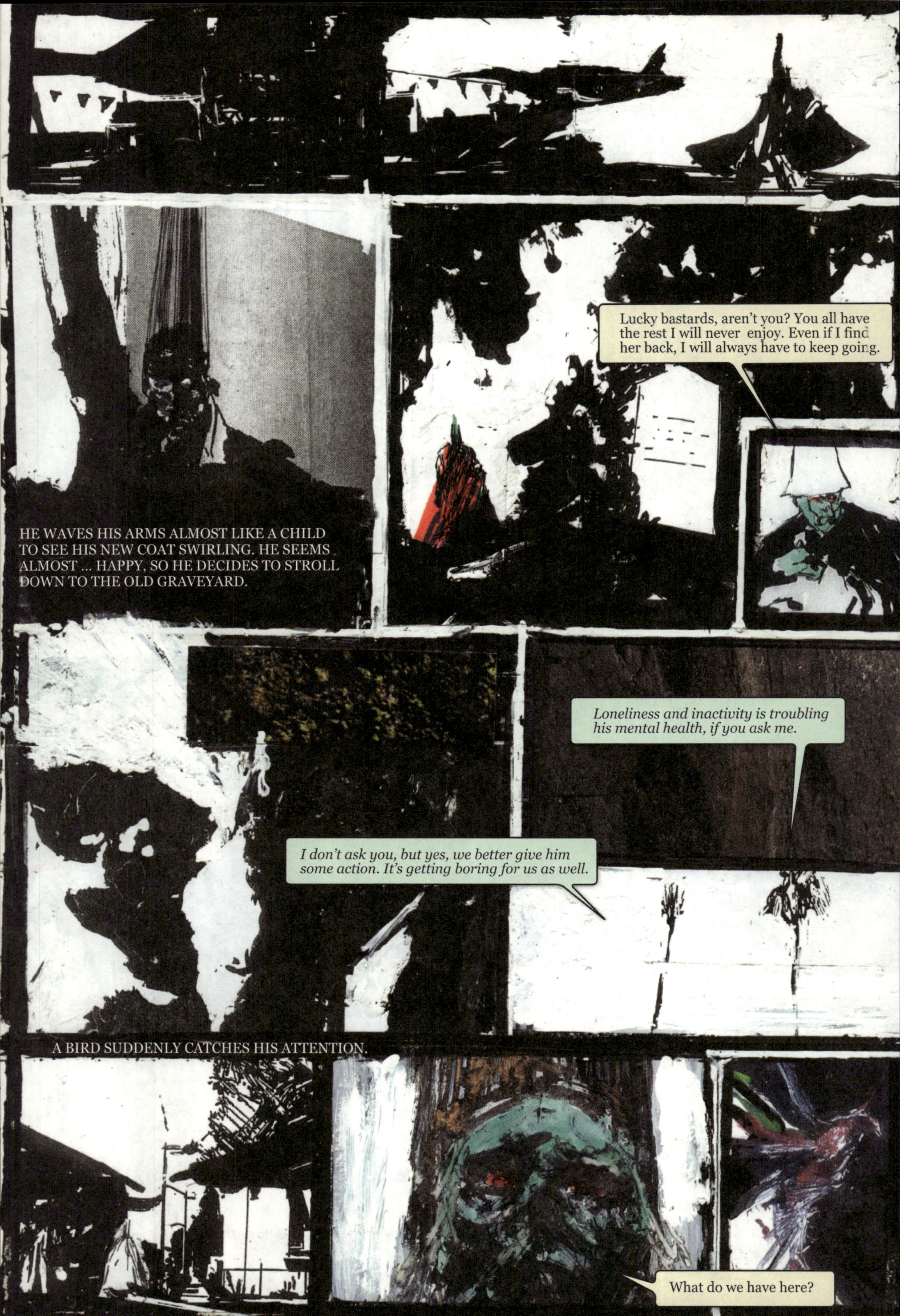

Lucky bastards, aren't you? You all have the rest I will never enjoy. Even if I find her back, I will always have to keep going.
HE WAVES HIS ARMS ALMOST LIKE A CHILD TO SEE HIS NEW COAT SWIRLING. HE SEEMS ALMOST ... HAPPY, SO HE DECIDES TO STROLL DOWN TO THE OLD GRAVEYARD.
Loneliness and inactivity is troubling his mental health, if you ask me.
I don't ask you, but yes, we better give him some action. It's getting boring for us as well.
A BIRD SUDDENLY CATCHES HIS ATTENTION.
What do we have here?

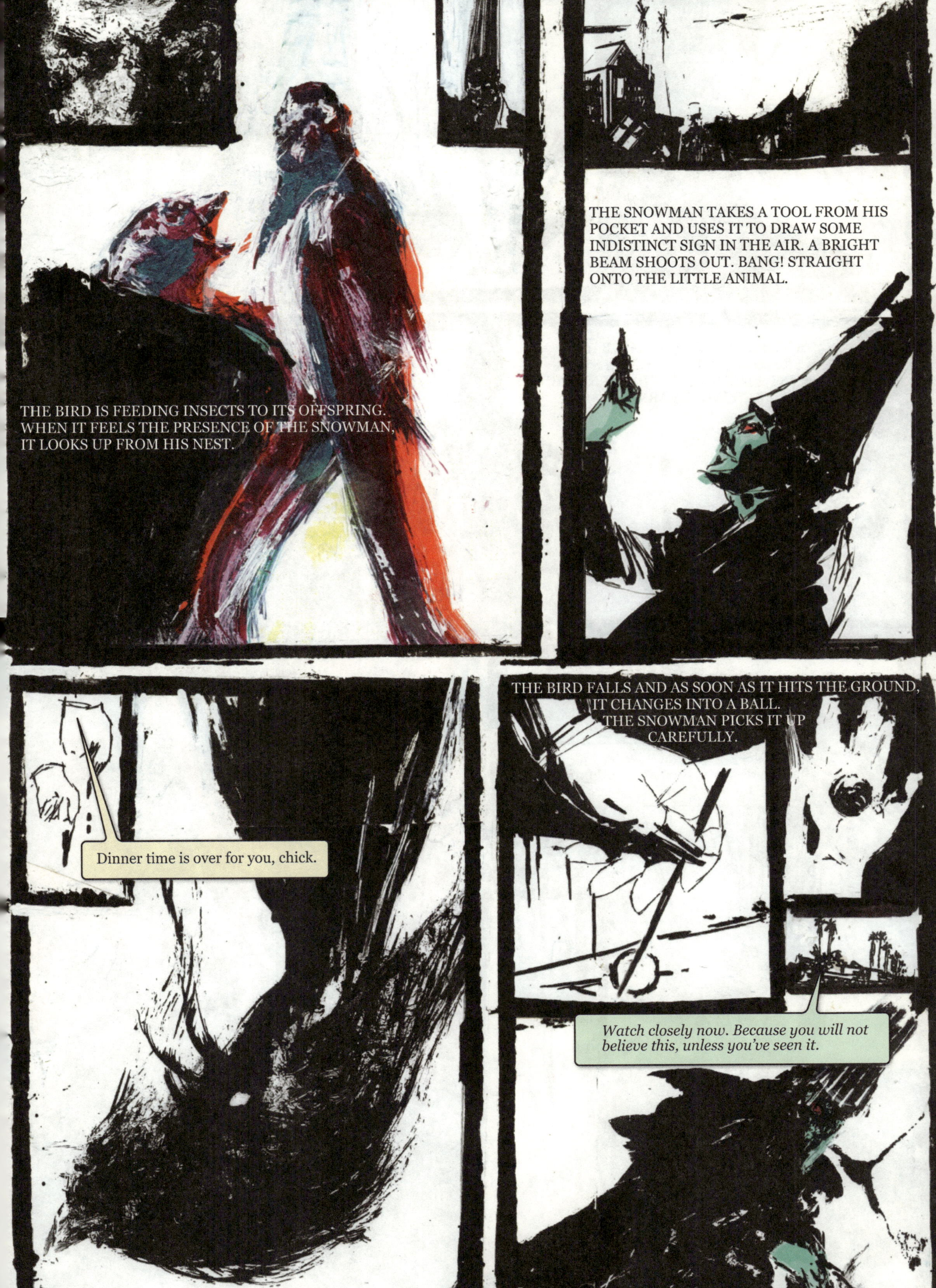
THE BIRD IS FEEDING INSECTS TO ITS OFFSPRING. WHEN IT FEELS THE PRESENCE OF THE SNOWMAN, IT LOOKS UP FROM HIS NEST.
THE SNOWMAN TAKES A TOOL FROM HIS POCKET AND USES IT TO DRAW SOME INDISTINCT SIGN IN THE AIR. A BRIGHT BEAM SHOOTS OUT. BANG! STRAIGHT ONTO THE LITTLE ANIMAL.
Dinner time is over for you, chick.
THE BIRD FALLS AND AS SOON AS IT HITS THE GROUND, IT CHANGES INTO A BALL. THE SNOWMAN PICKS IT UP CAREFULLY.
Watch closely now. Because you will not believe this, unless you've seen it.

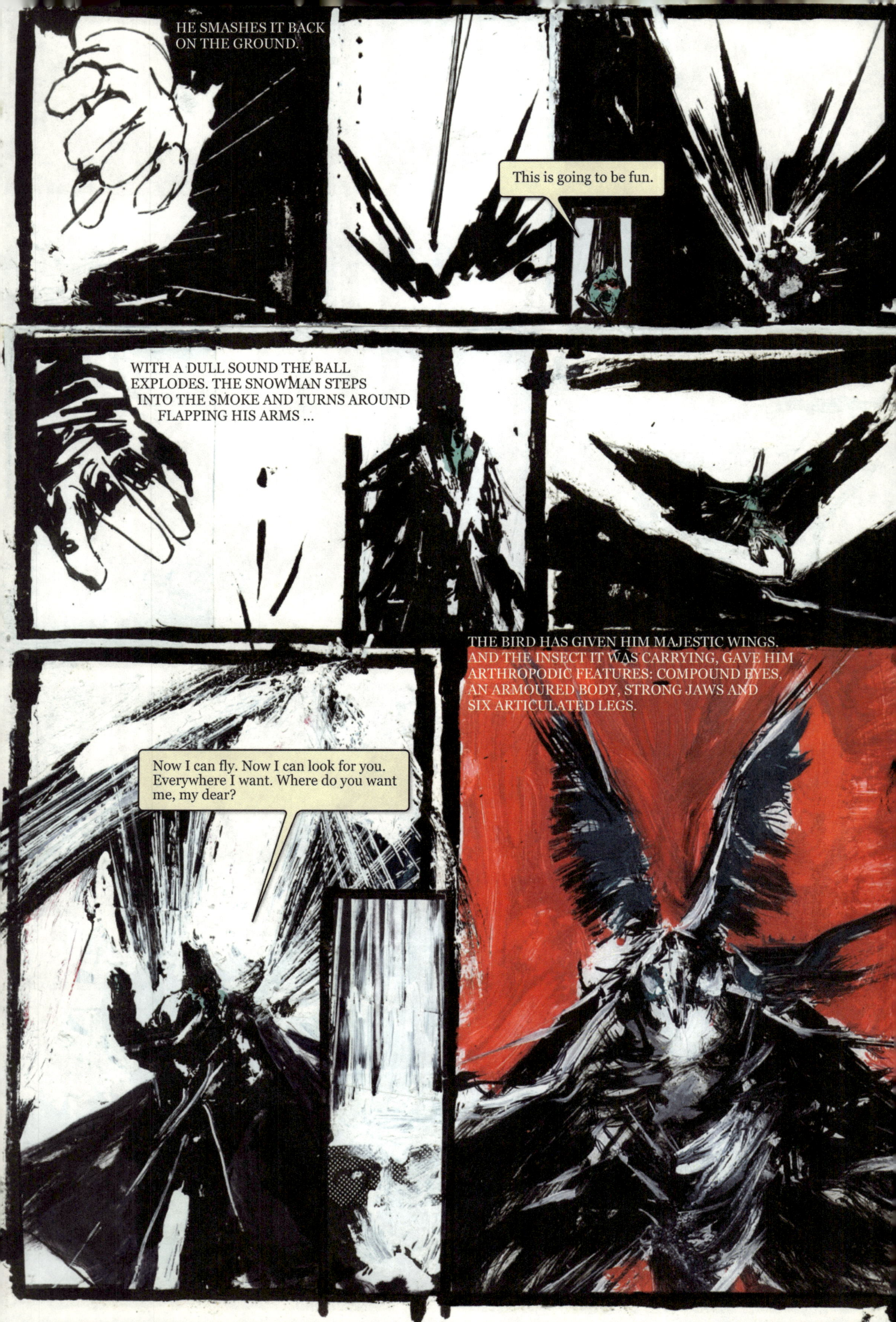

HE SMASHES IT BACK ON THE GROUND.
This is going to be fun.
WITH A DULL SOUND THE BALL EXPLODES. THE SNOWMAN STEPS INTO THE SMOKE AND TURNS AROUND FLAPPING HIS ARMS ...
THE BIRD HAS GIVEN HIM MAJESTIC WINGS. AND THE INSECT IT WAS CARRYING, GAVE HIM ARTHROPODIC FEATURES: COMPOUND EYES, AN ARMOURED BODY, STRONG JAWS AND SIX ARTICULATED LEGS.
Now I can fly. Now I can look for you. Everywhere I want. Where do you want me, my dear?

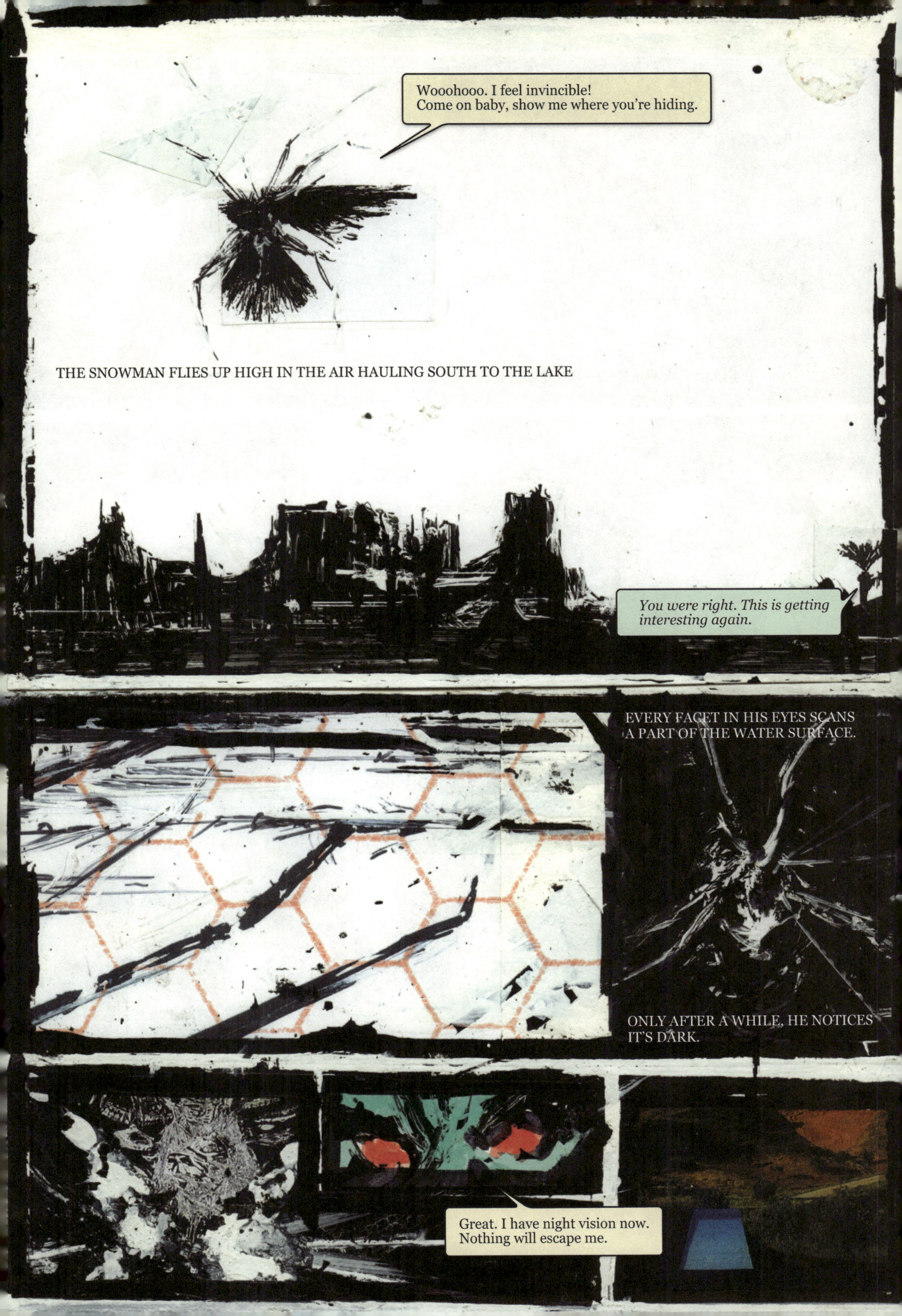

THE SNOWMAN FLIES UP HIGH IN THE AIR HAULING SOUTH TO THE LAKE

EVERY FACET IN HIS EYES SCANS A PART OF THE WATER SURFACE.

ONLY AFTER A WHILE, HE NOTICES IT'S DARK.

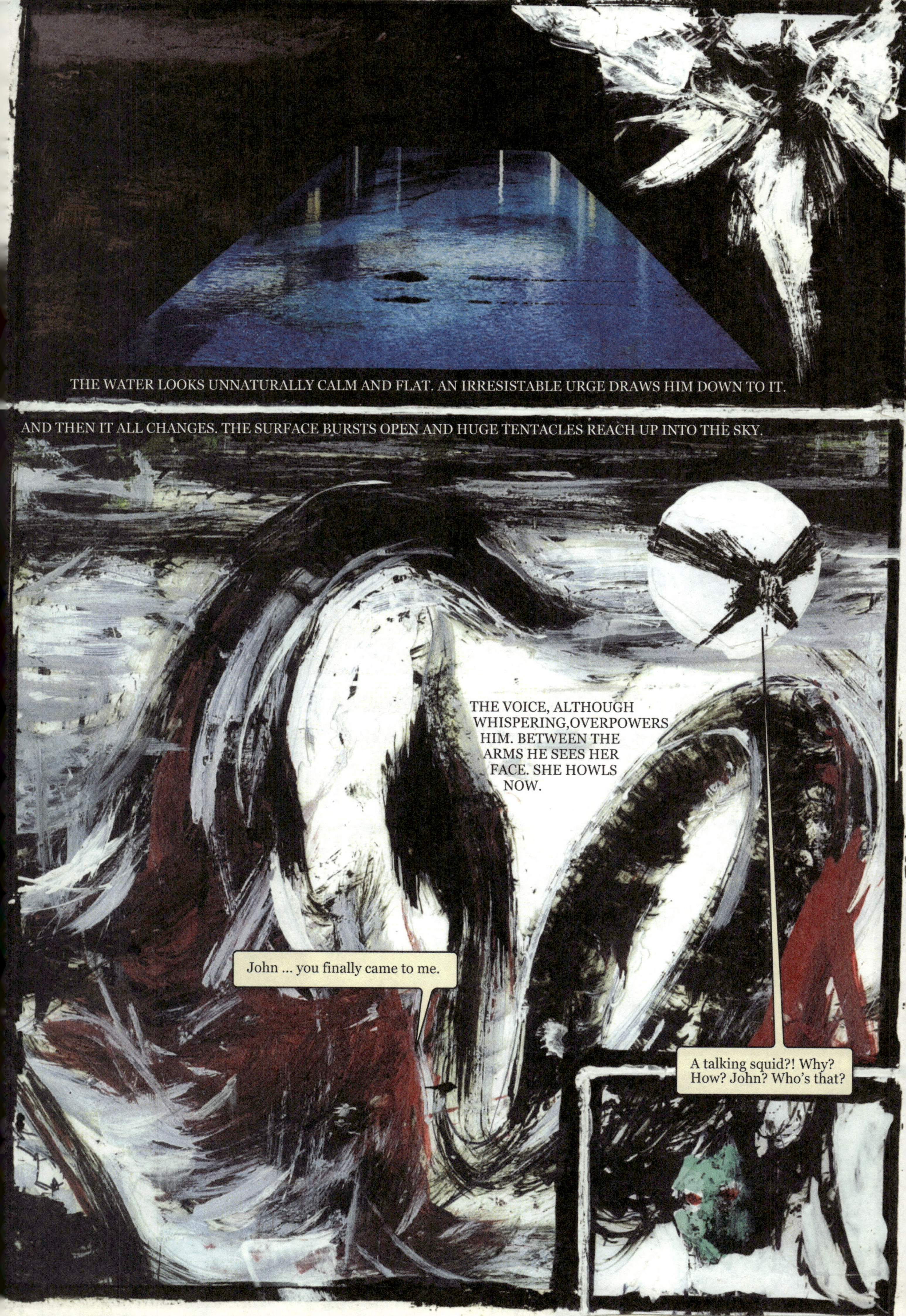

THE WATER LOOKS UNNATURALLY CALM AND FLAT. AN IRRESISTABLE URGE DRAWS HIM DOWN TO IT.
AND THEN IT ALL CHANGES. THE SURFACE BURSTS OPEN AND HUGE TENTACLES REACH UP INTO THE SKY.
THE VOICE, ALTHOUGH WHISPERING,OVERPOWERS HIM. BETWEEN THE ARMS HE SEES HER FACE. SHE HOWLS NOW.
John ... you finally came to me.
A talking squid?! Why? How? John? Who's that?

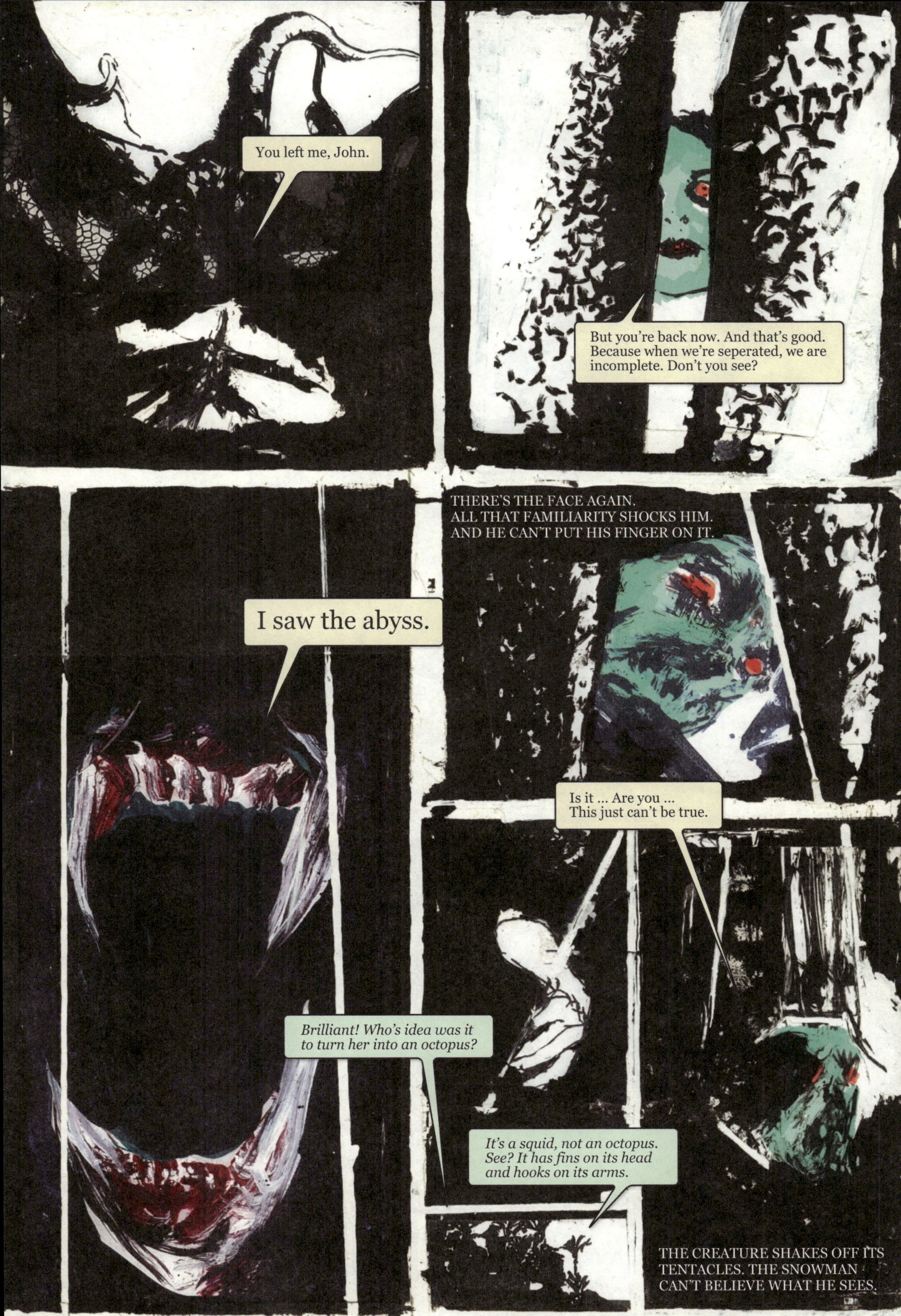

You left me, John.
But you're back now. And that's good. Because when we're seperated, we are incomplete. Don't you see?
THERE'S THE FACE AGAIN. ALL THAT FAMILIARITY SHOCKS HIM. AND HE CAN'T PUT HIS FINGER ON IT.
I saw the abyss.
Is it ... Are you ... This just can't be true.
Brilliant! Who's idea was it to turn her into an octopus?
It's a squid, not an octopus. See? It has fins on its head and hooks on its arms.
THE CREATURE SHAKES OFF ITS TENTACLES. THE SNOWMAN CAN'T BELIEVE WHAT HE SEES.

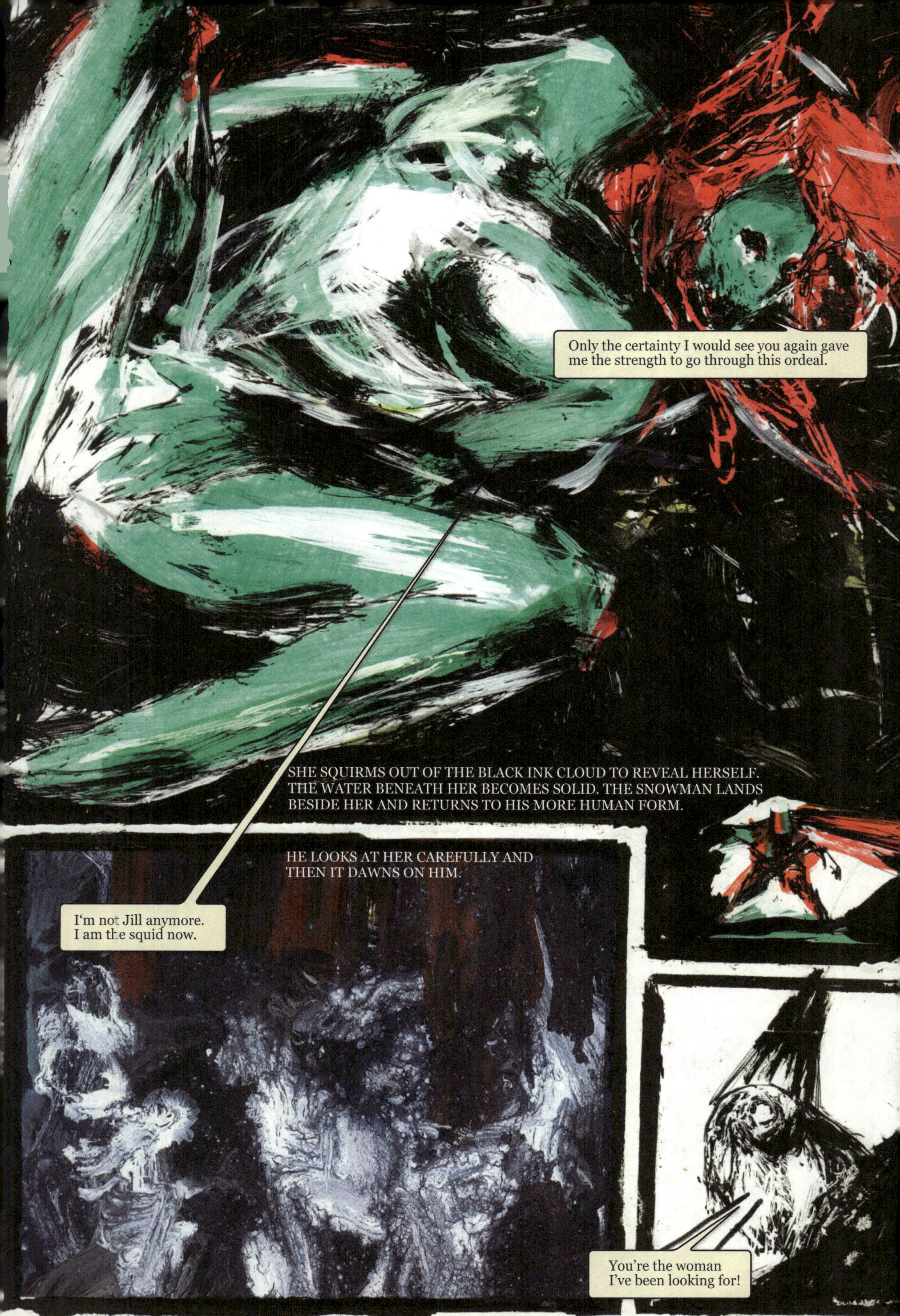
Only the certainty I would see you again gave me the strength to go through this ordeal.
SHE SQUIRMS OUT OF THE BLACK INK CLOUD TO REVEAL HERSELF. THE WATER BENEATH HER BECOMES SOLID. THE SNOWMAN LANDS BESIDE HER AND RETURNS TO HIS MORE HUMAN FORM.
HE LOOKS AT HER CAREFULLY AND THEN IT DAWNS ON HIM.
I'm not Jill anymore. I am the squid now.
You're the woman I've been looking for!

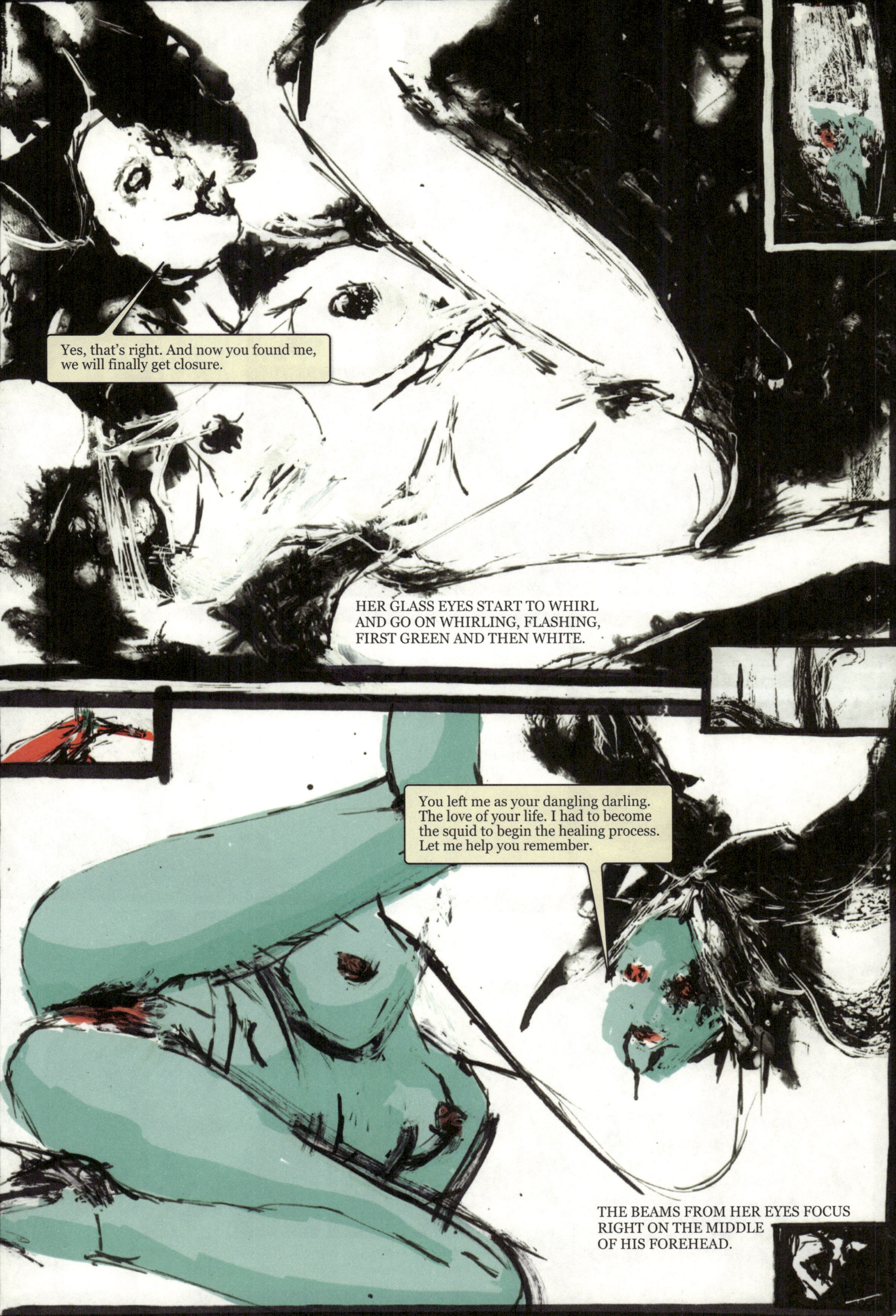

Yes, that's right. And now you found me, we will finally get closure.
HER GLASS EYES START TO WHIRL AND GO ON WHIRLING, FLASHING, FIRST GREEN AND THEN WHITE.
You left me as your dangling darling. The love of your life. I had to become the squid to begin the healing process. Let me help you remember.
THE BEAMS FROM HER EYES FOCUS RIGHT ON THE MIDDLE OF HIS FOREHEAD.

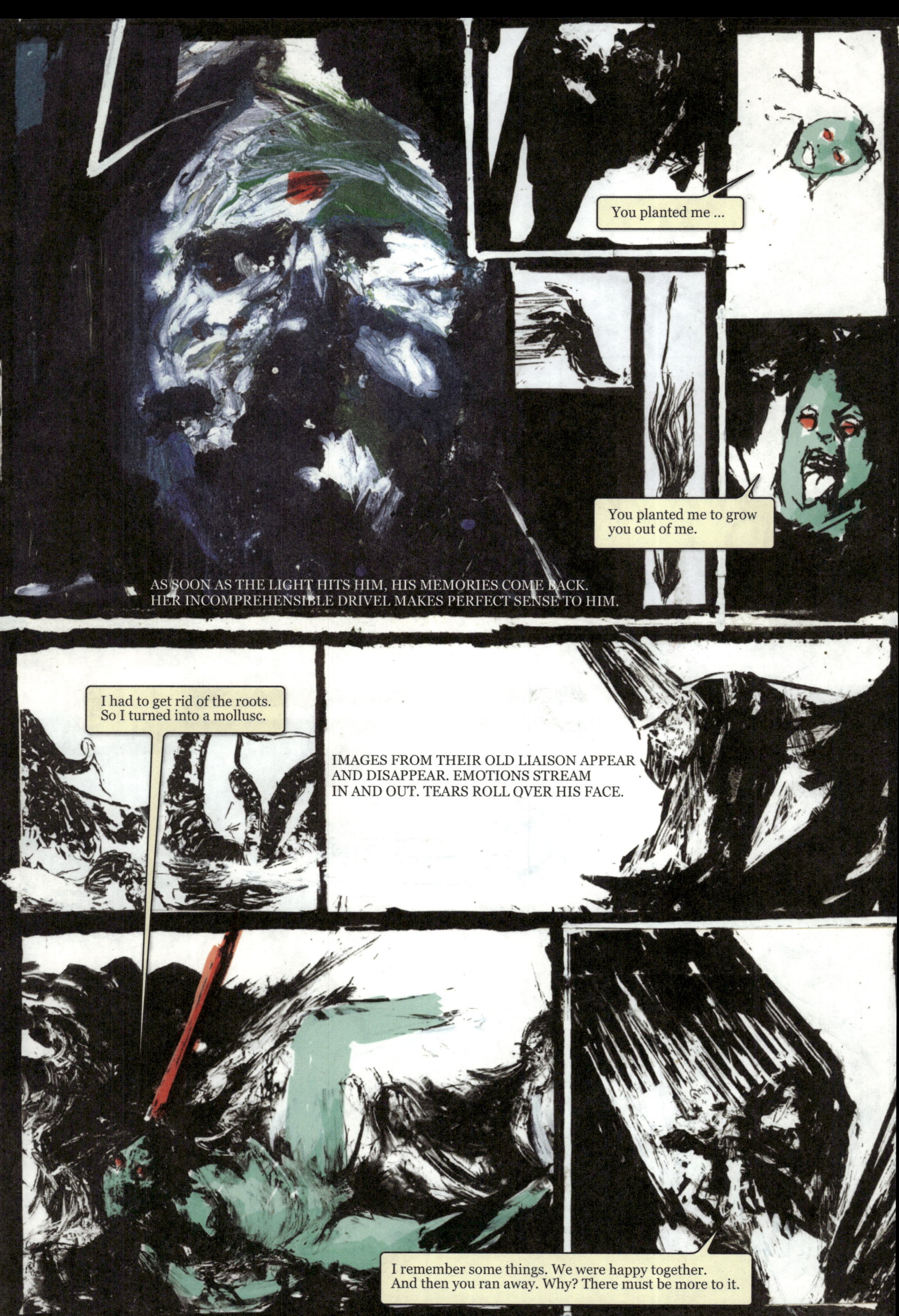

You planted me ...
You planted me to grow you out of me.
AS SOON AS THE LIGHT HITS HIM, HIS MEMORIES COME BACK.
HER INCOMPREHENSIBLE DRIVEL MAKES PERFECT SENSE TO HIM.
I had to get rid of the roots.
So I turned into a mollusc.
IMAGES FROM THEIR OLD LIAISON APPEAR
AND DISAPPEAR. EMOTIONS STREAM
IN AND OUT. TEARS ROLL OVER HIS FACE.
I remember some things. We were happy together.
And then you ran away. Why? There must be more to it.

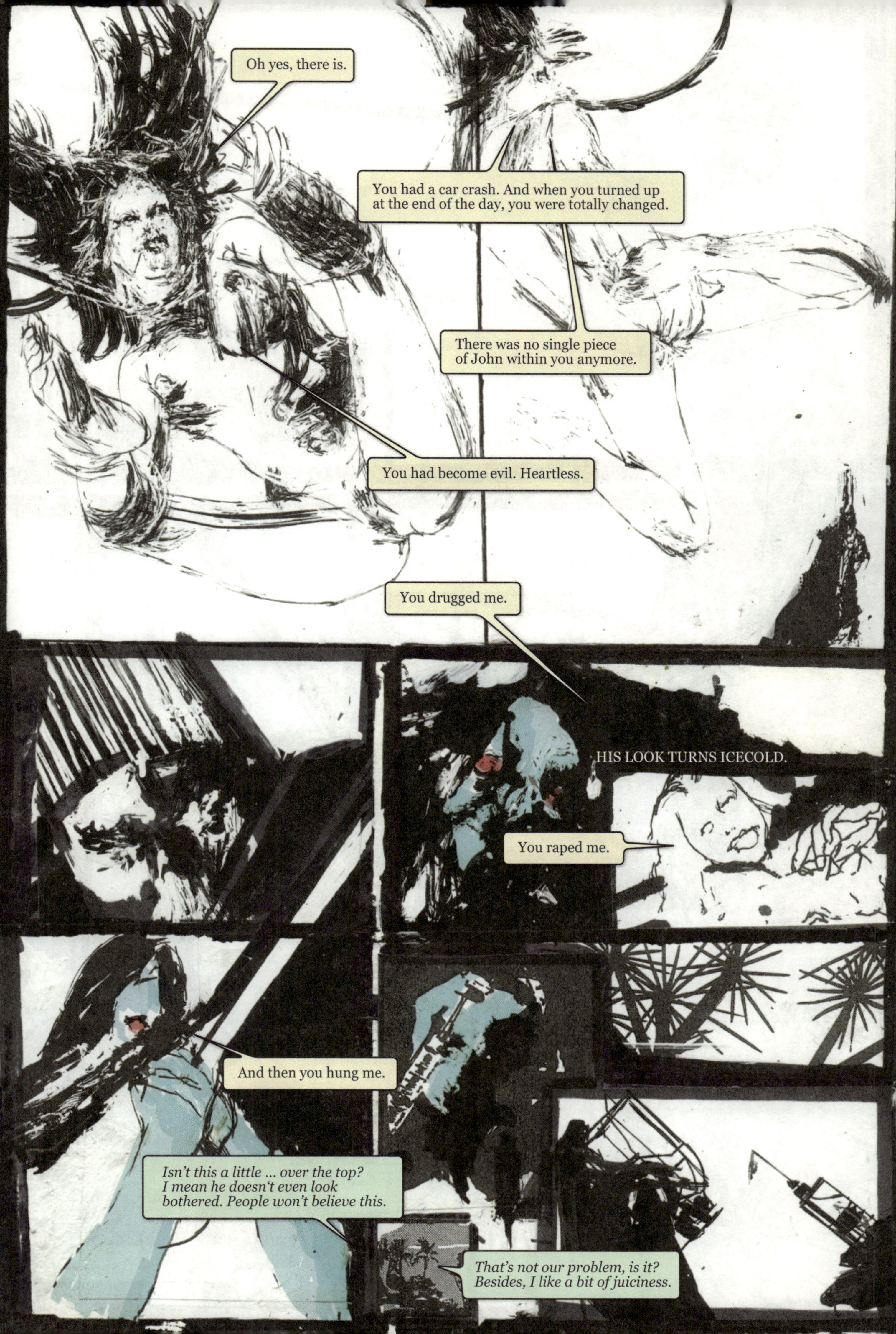

Oh yes, there is.
You had a car crash. And when you turned up at the end of the day, you were totally changed.
There was no single piece of John within you anymore.
You had become evil. Heartless.
You drugged me.
HIS LOOK TURNS ICECOLD.
You raped me.
And then you hung me.
Isn't this a little ... over the top? I mean he doesn't even look bothered. People won't believe this.
That's not our problem, is it? Besides, I like a bit of juiciness.

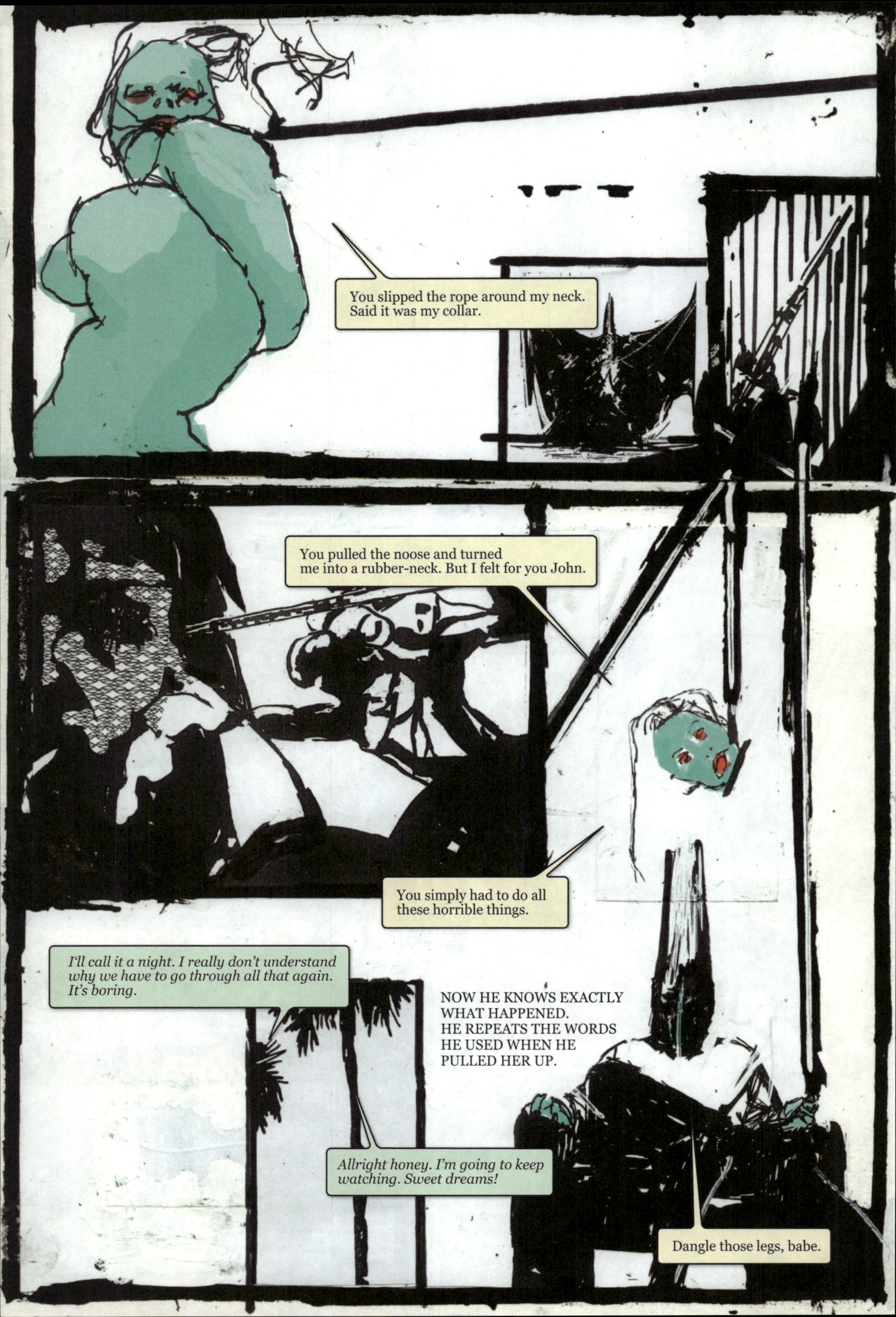

You slipped the rope around my neck. Said it was my collar.
You pulled the noose and turned me into a rubber-neck. But I felt for you John.
You simply had to do all these horrible things.
I'll call it a night. I really don't understand why we have to go through all that again. It's boring.
NOW HE KNOWS EXACTLY WHAT HAPPENED. HE REPEATS THE WORDS HE USED WHEN HE PULLED HER UP.
Allright honey. I'm going to keep watching. Sweet dreams!
Dangle those legs, babe.

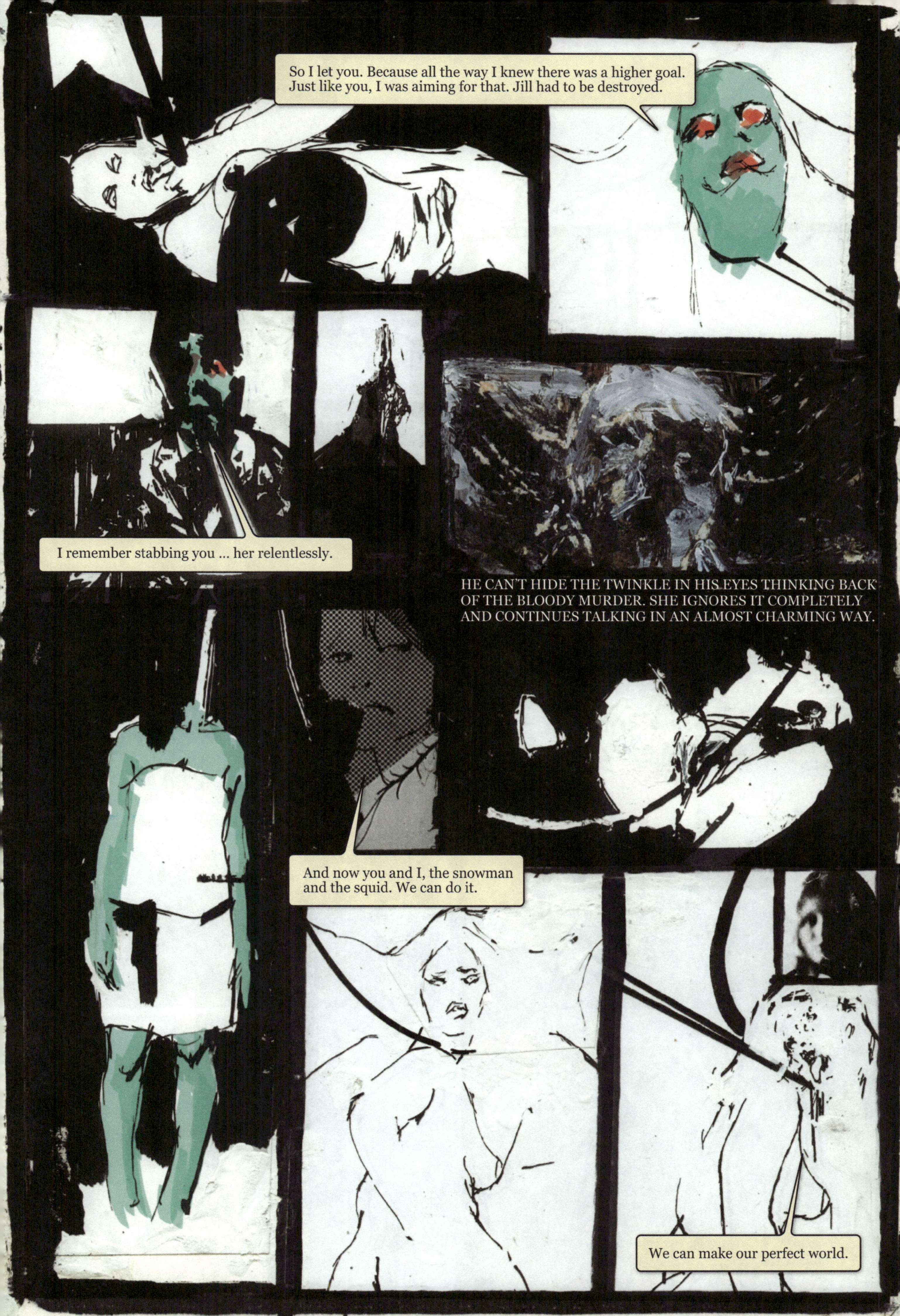

So I let you. Because all the way I knew there was a higher goal. Just like you, I was aiming for that. Jill had to be destroyed.
I remember stabbing you ... her relentlessly.
HE CAN'T HIDE THE TWINKLE IN HIS EYES THINKING BACK OF THE BLOODY MURDER. SHE IGNORES IT COMPLETELY AND CONTINUES TALKING IN AN ALMOST CHARMING WAY.
And now you and I, the snowman and the squid. We can do it.
We can make our perfect world.

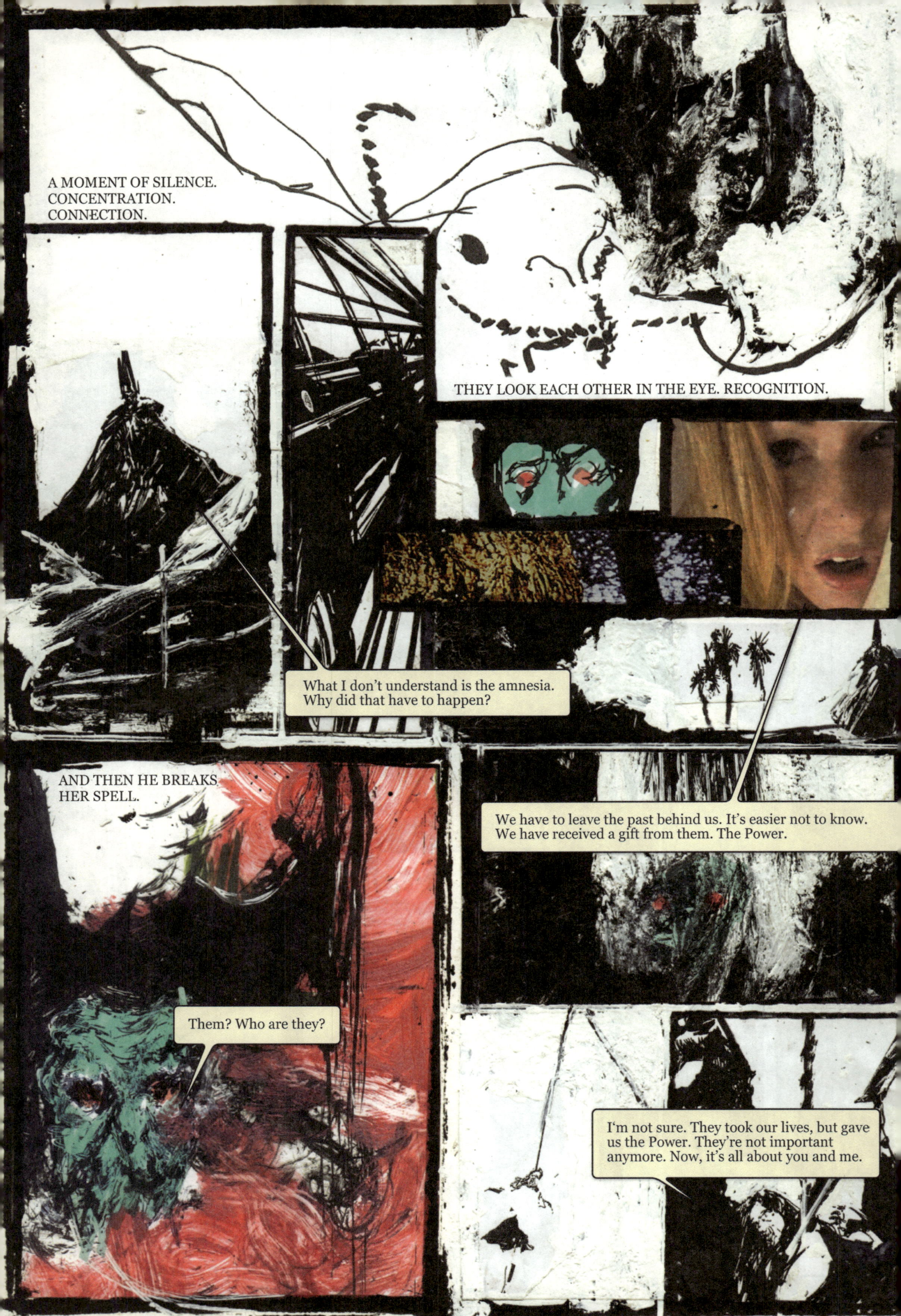

A MOMENT OF SILENCE.
CONCENTRATION.
CONNECTION.
THEY LOOK EACH OTHER IN THE EYE. RECOGNITION.
What I don't understand is the amnesia. Why did that have to happen?
AND THEN HE BREAKS HER SPELL.
We have to leave the past behind us. It's easier not to know. We have received a gift from them. The Power.
Them? Who are they?
I'm not sure. They took our lives, but gave us the Power. They're not important anymore. Now, it's all about you and me.

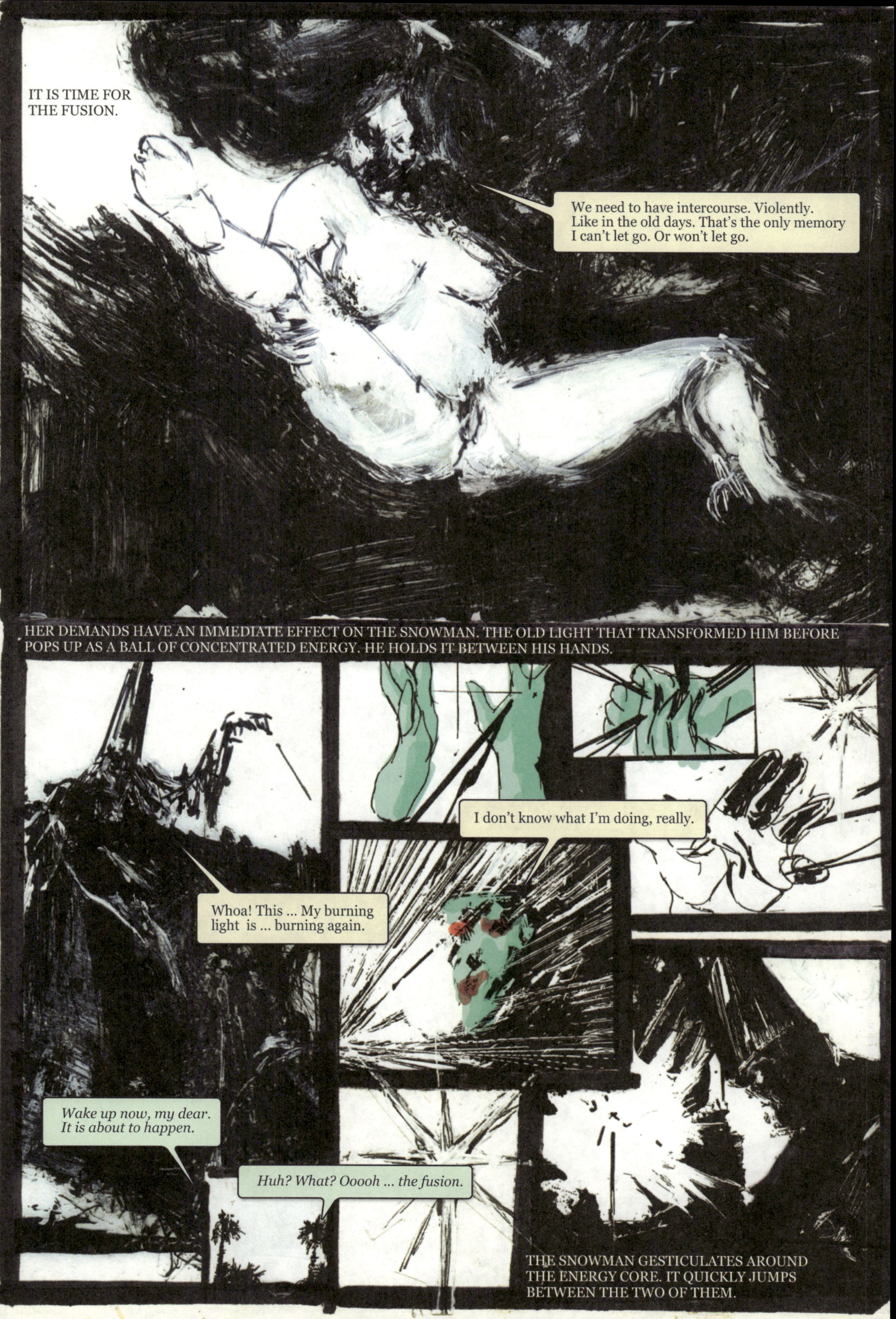

IT IS TIME FOR THE FUSION.
We need to have intercourse. Violently. Like in the old days. That's the only memory I can't let go. Or won't let go.
HER DEMANDS HAVE AN IMMEDIATE EFFECT ON THE SNOWMAN. THE OLD LIGHT THAT TRANSFORMED HIM BEFORE POPS UP AS A BALL OF CONCENTRATED ENERGY. HE HOLDS IT BETWEEN HIS HANDS.
I don't know what I'm doing, really.
Whoa! This ... My burning light is ... burning again.
Wake up now, my dear. It is about to happen.
Huh? What? Ooooh ... the fusion.
THE SNOWMAN GESTICULATES AROUND THE ENERGY CORE. IT QUICKLY JUMPS BETWEEN THE TWO OF THEM.

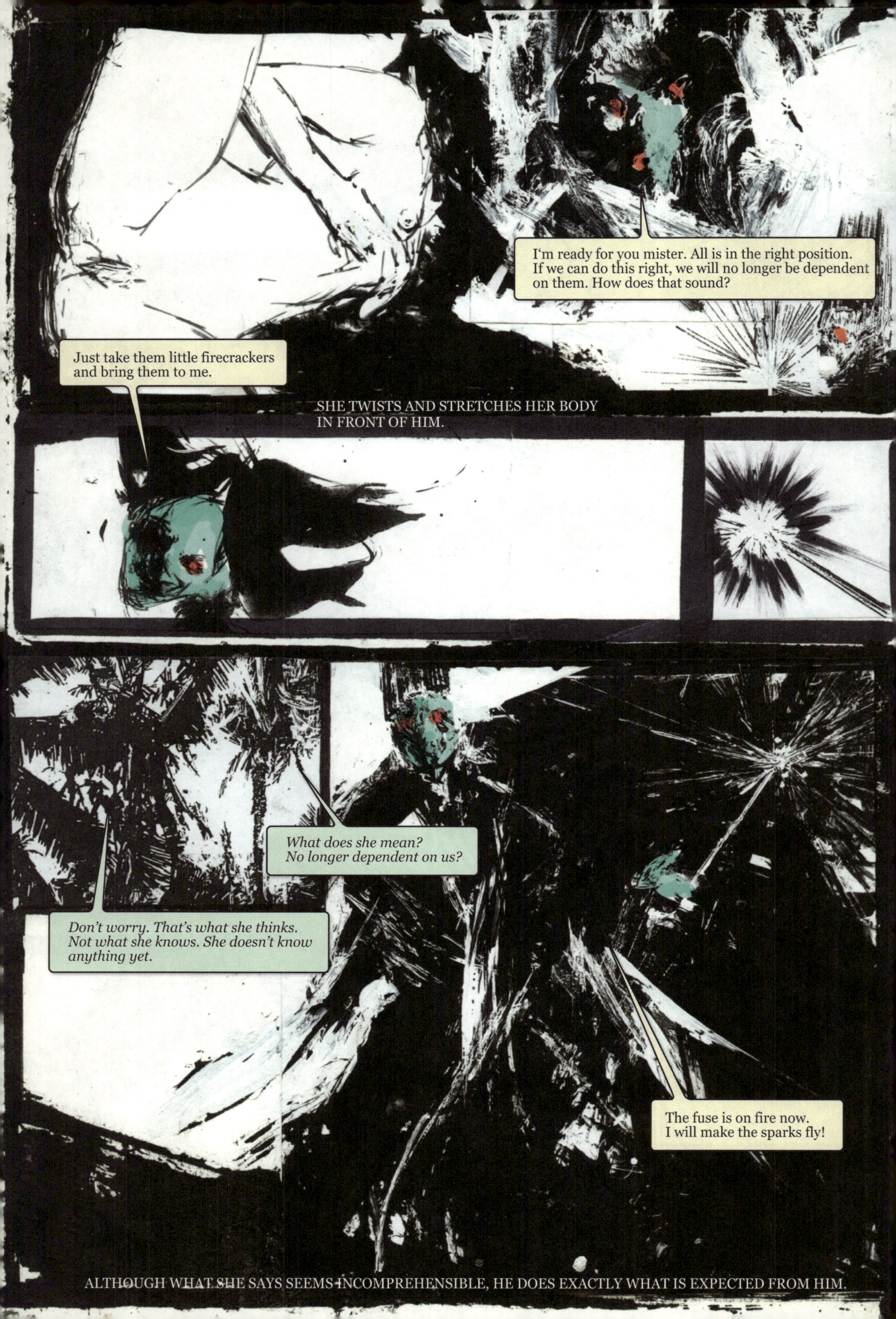

SHE TWISTS AND STRETCHES HER BODY IN FRONT OF HIM.

ALTHOUGH WHAT SHE SAYS SEEMS INCOMPREHENSIBLE, HE DOES EXACTLY WHAT IS EXPECTED FROM HIM.

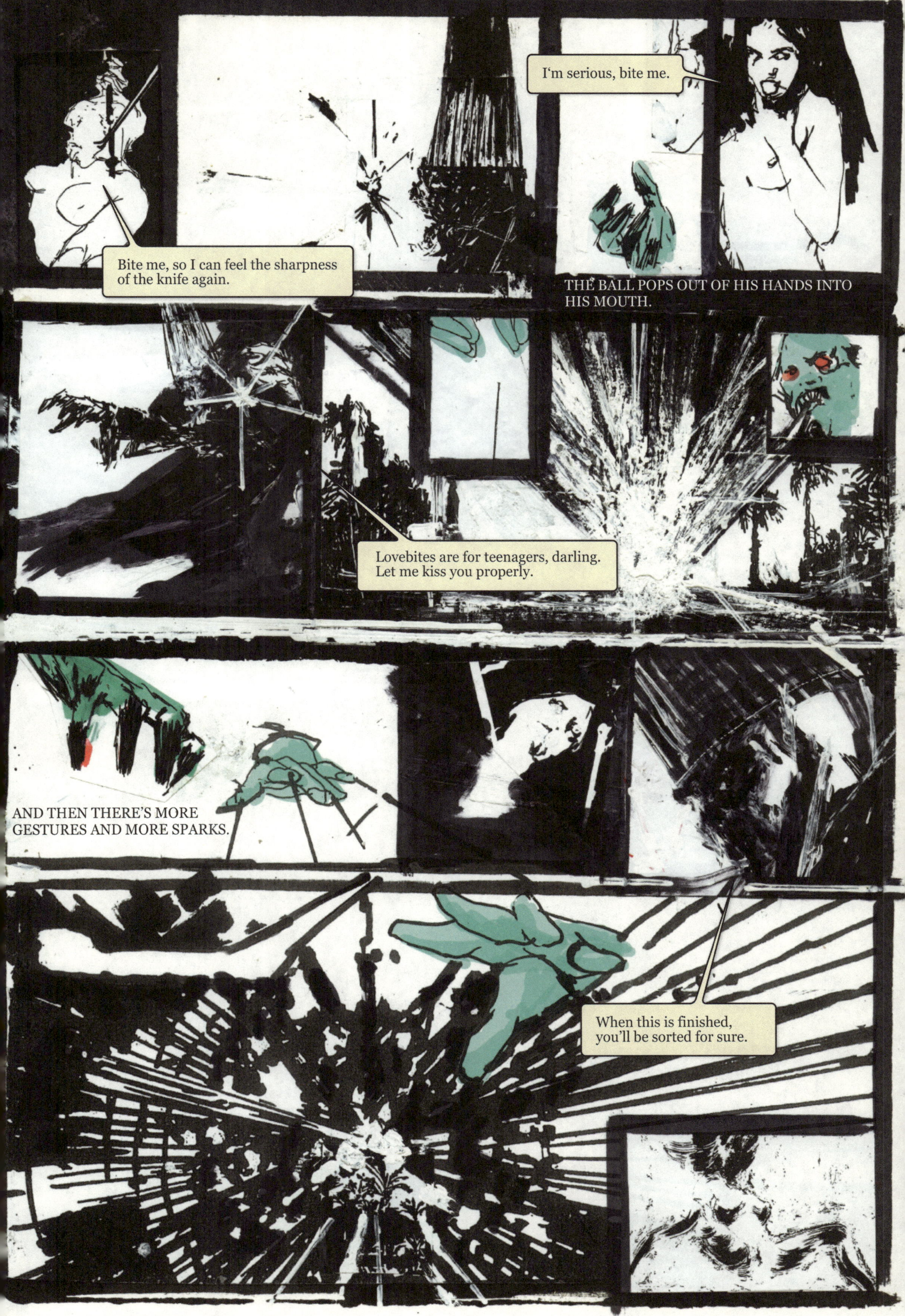

I'm serious, bite me.
Bite me, so I can feel the sharpness of the knife again.
THE BALL POPS OUT OF HIS HANDS INTO HIS MOUTH.
Lovebites are for teenagers, darling. Let me kiss you properly.
AND THEN THERE'S MORE GESTURES AND MORE SPARKS.
When this is finished, you'll be sorted for sure.

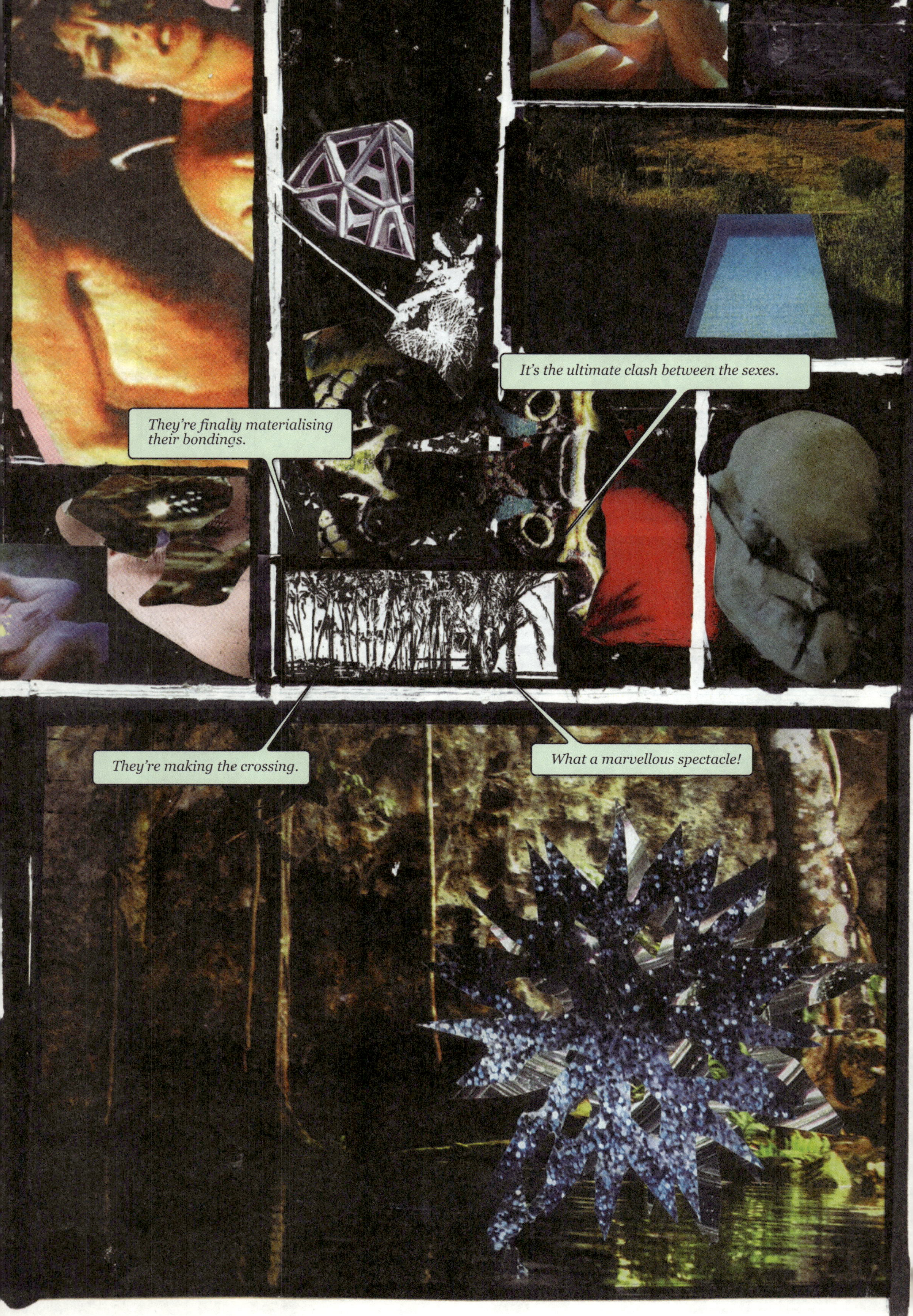
They're finally materialising their bondings.
It's the ultimate clash between the sexes.
They're making the crossing.
What a marvellous spectacle!

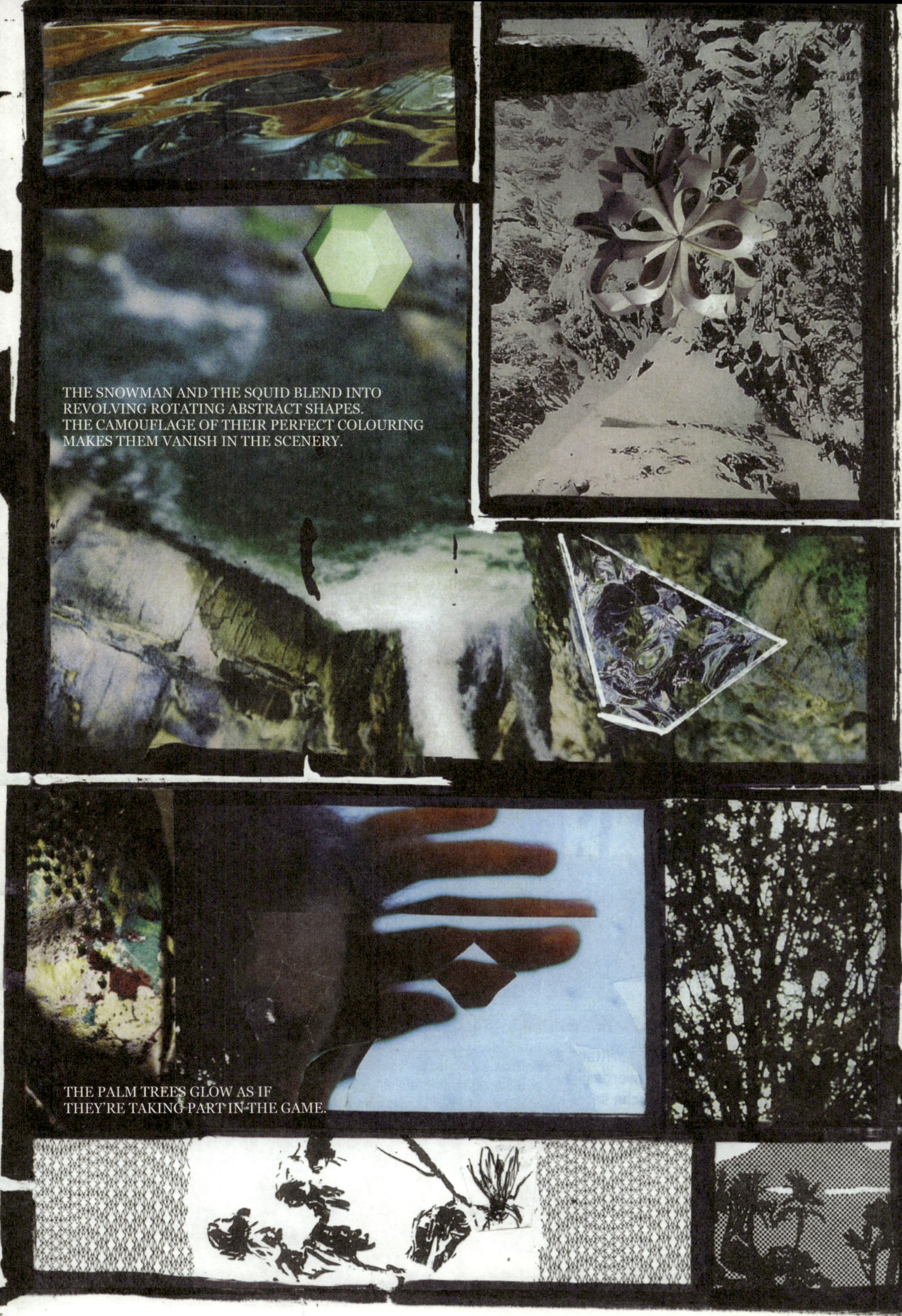

THE SNOWMAN AND THE SQUID BLEND INTO
REVOLVING ROTATING ABSTRACT SHAPES.
THE CAMOUFLAGE OF THEIR PERFECT COLOURING
MAKES THEM VANISH IN THE SCENERY.
THE PALM TREES GLOW AS IF
THEY'RE TAKING PART IN THE GAME.

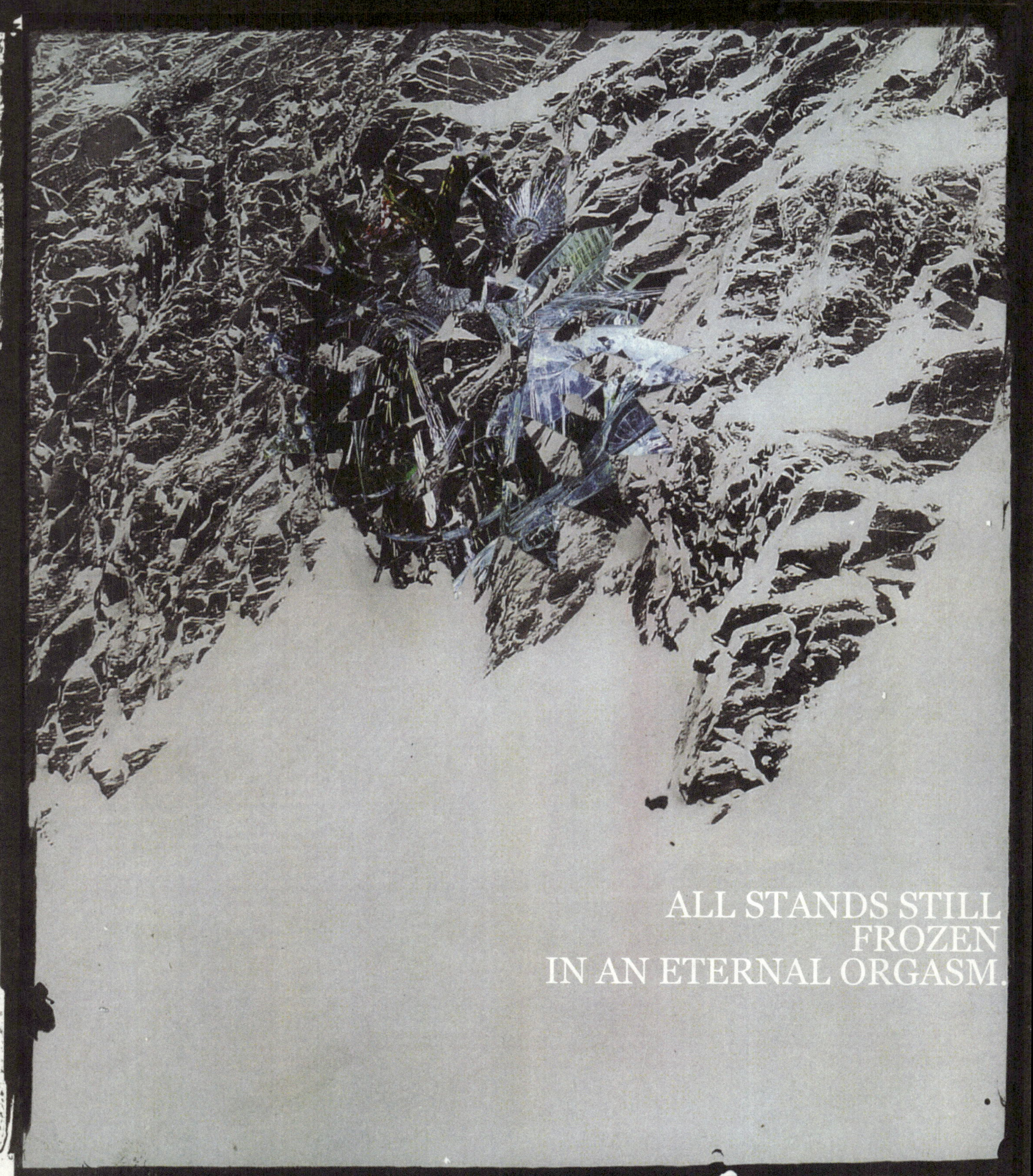

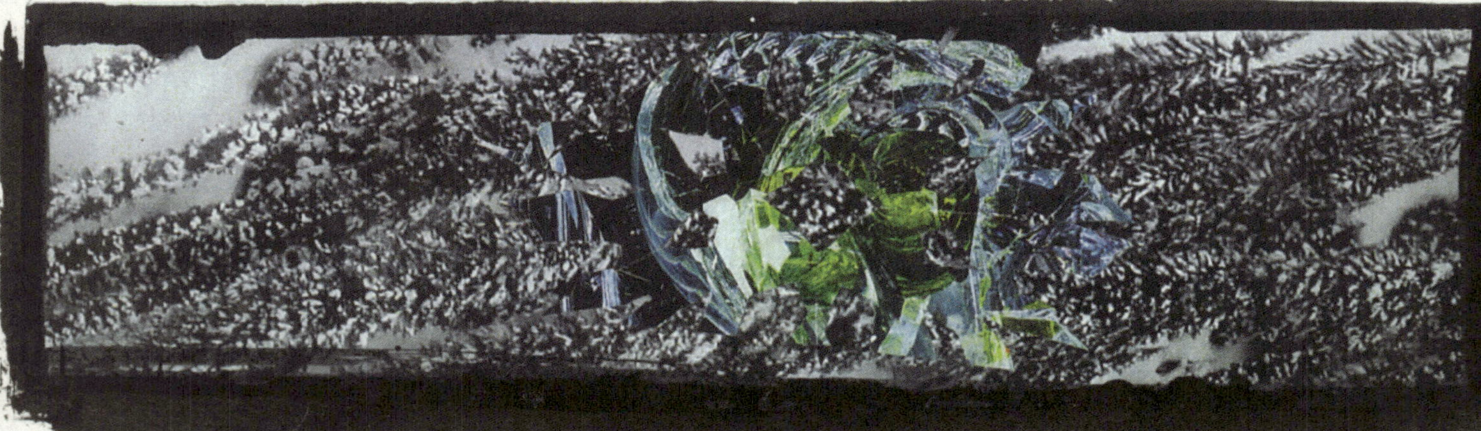

ALL STANDS STILL
FROZEN
IN AN ETERNAL ORGASM.

TOTALLY AT PEACE WITH THEIR NEW UNIVERSE, THE SNOWMAN AND THE SQUID FLOAT AWAY. TINY PARTICLES OF SPACECUM DANCE AROUND THEM IN THE AIR UNTIL THEY CLOT INTO ONE CRYSTAL. SEPERATION HAS BECOME INEVITABLE. THEY HAVE TO BRING THE EARTH BACK INTO ITS NATURAL CONDITION OR IT WILL BE LOST FOREVER.

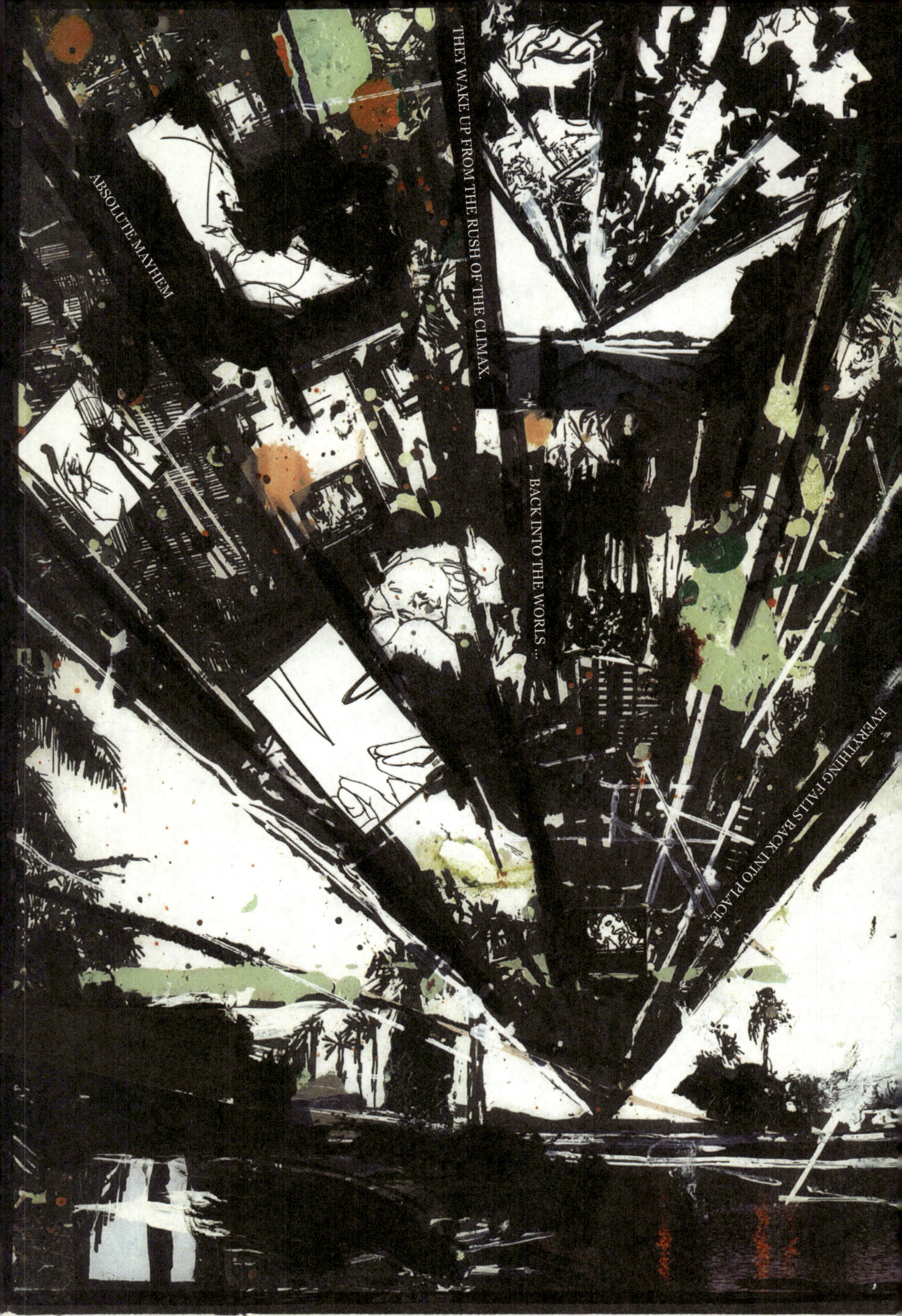

ABSOLUTE MAYHEM
THEY WAKE UP FROM THE RUSH OF THE CLIMAX
BACK INTO THE WORLS ...
EVERYTHING FALLS BACK INTO PLACE

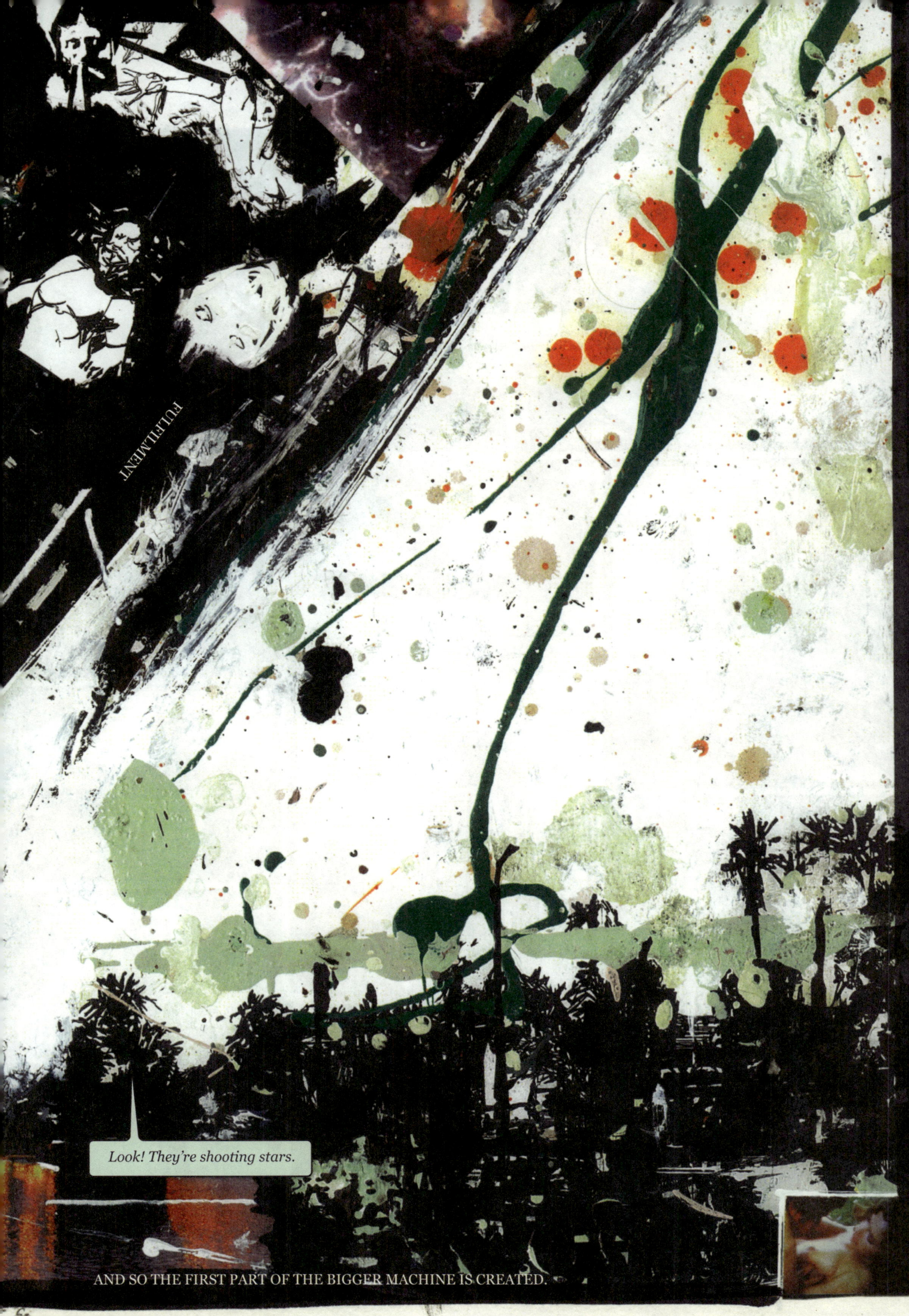
FULFILMENT
Look! They're shooting stars.
AND SO THE FIRST PART OF THE BIGGER MACHINE IS CREATED.

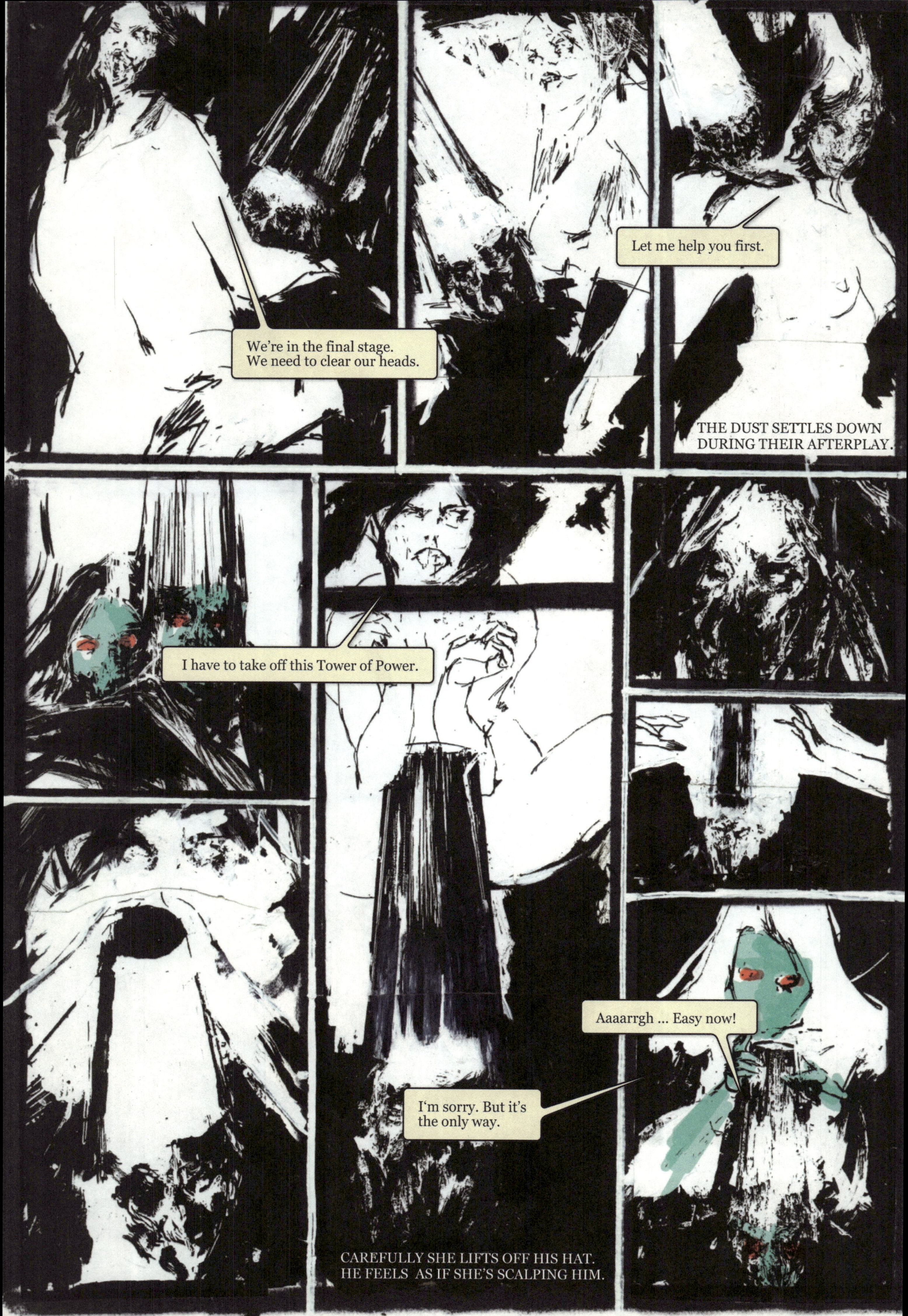
Let me help you first.
We're in the final stage.
We need to clear our heads.
THE DUST SETTLES DOWN
DURING THEIR AFTERPLAY.
I have to take off this Tower of Power.
Aaaarrgh ... Easy now!
I'm sorry. But it's
the only way.
CAREFULLY SHE LIFTS OFF HIS HAT.
HE FEELS AS IF SHE'S SCALPING HIM.

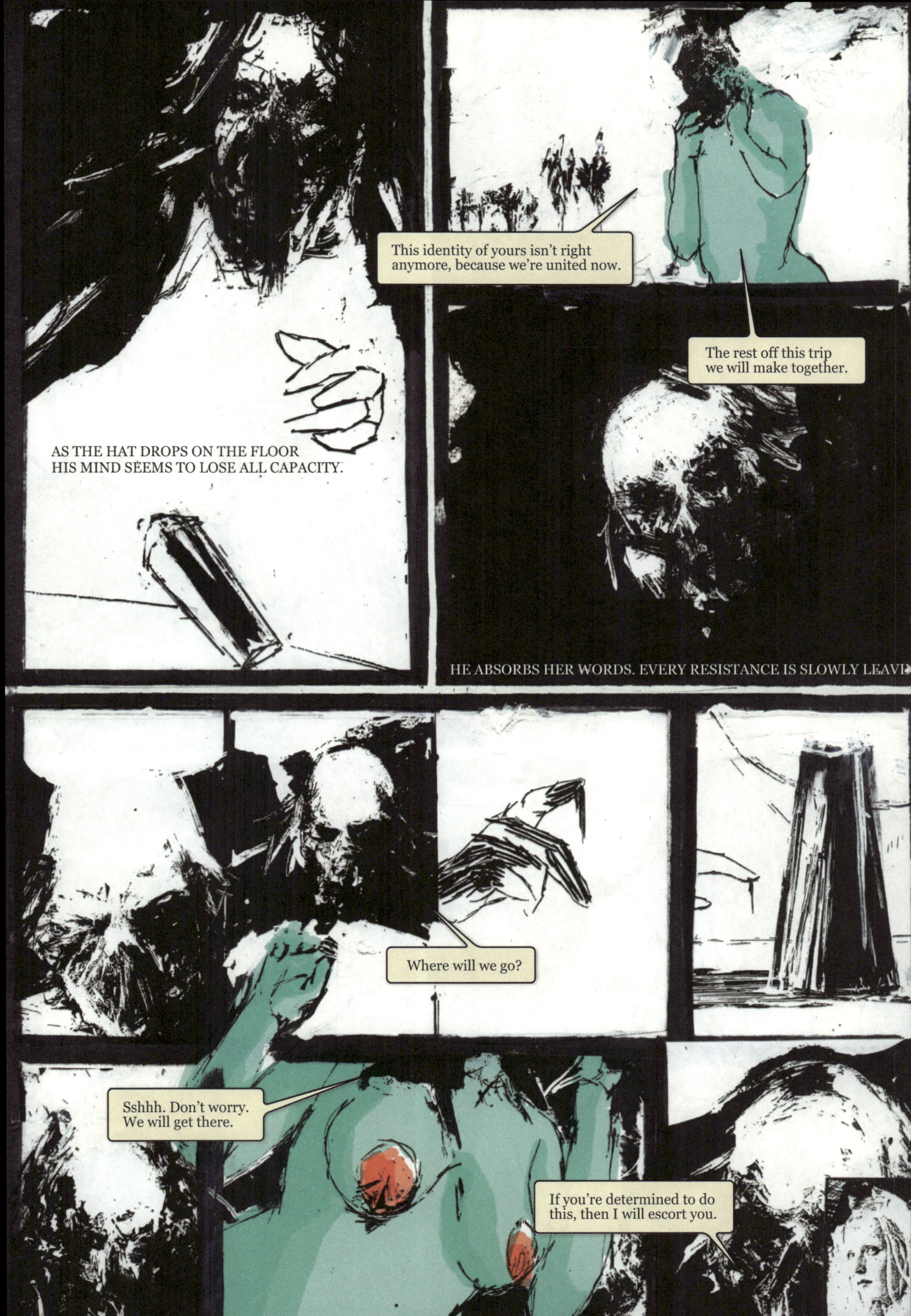

This identity of yours isn't right anymore, because we're united now.
The rest off this trip we will make together.
AS THE HAT DROPS ON THE FLOOR HIS MIND SEEMS TO LOSE ALL CAPACITY.
HE ABSORBS HER WORDS. EVERY RESISTANCE IS SLOWLY LEAVI
Where will we go?
Sshhh. Don't worry. We will get there.
If you're determined to do this, then I will escort you.

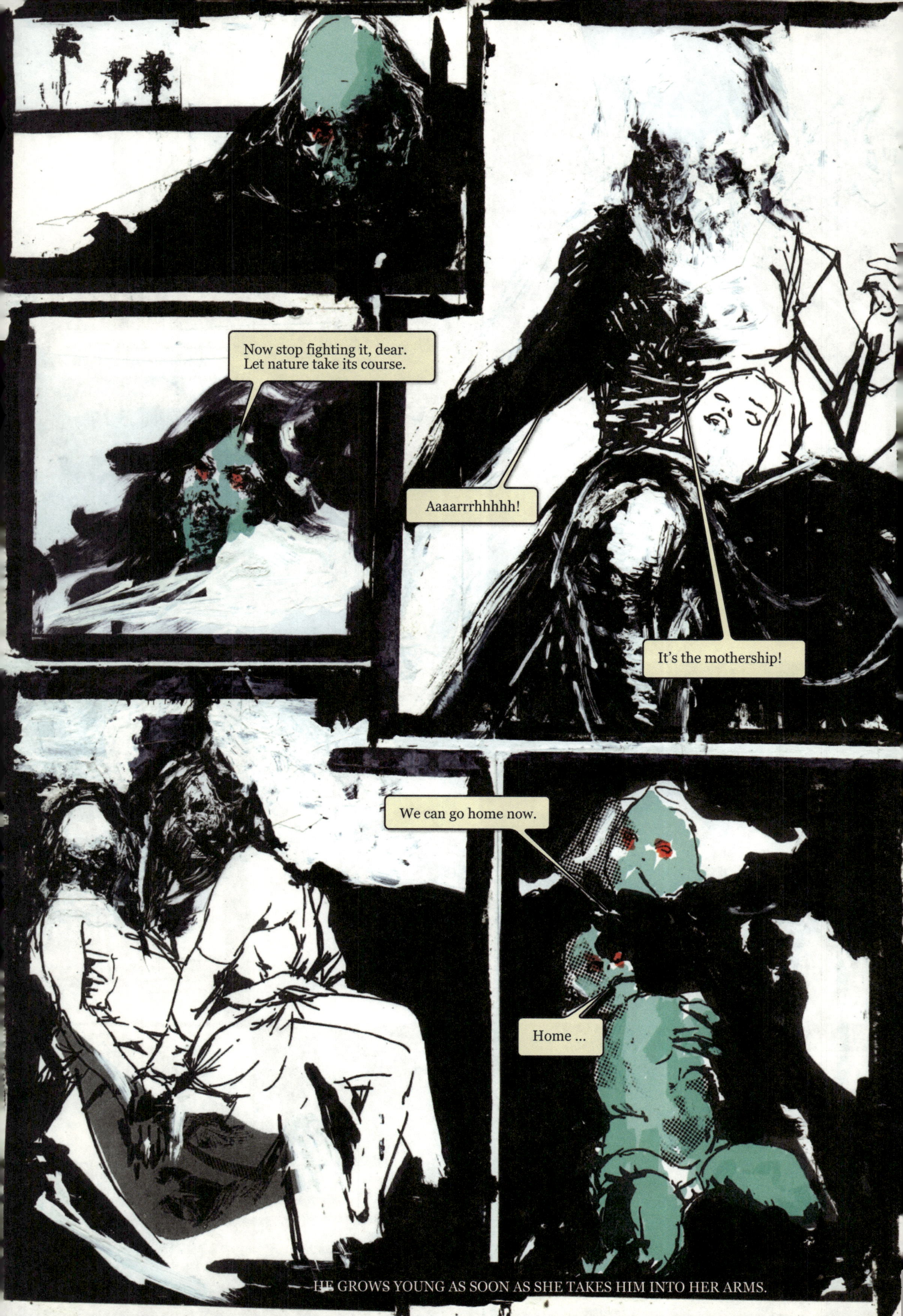

HE GROWS YOUNG AS SOON AS SHE TAKES HIM INTO HER ARMS.

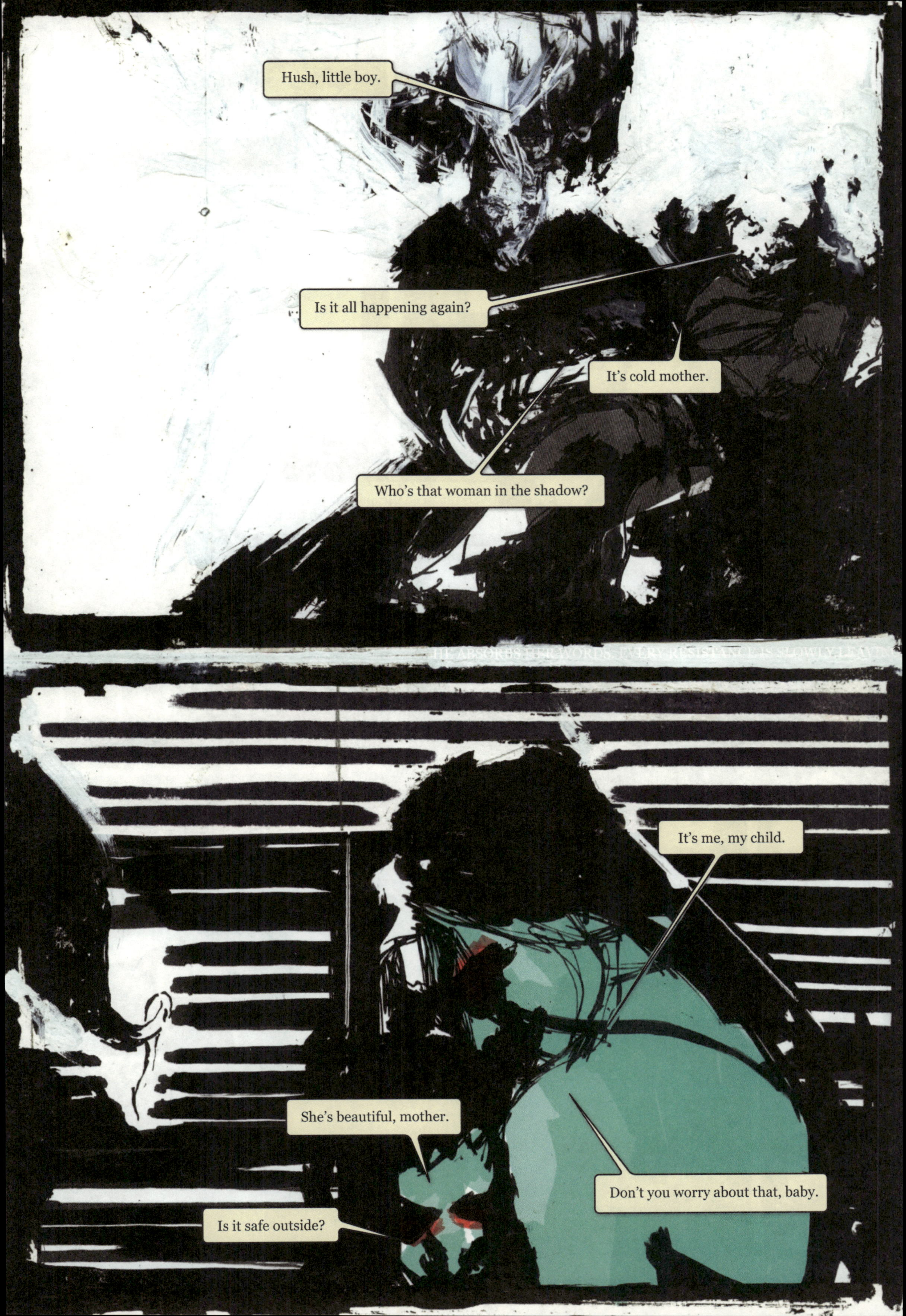

Hush, little boy.
Is it all happening again?
It's cold mother.
Who's that woman in the shadow?
HE ABSORBS HER WORDS. EVERY RESISTANCE IS SLOWLY LEAVING
It's me, my child.
She's beautiful, mother.
Don't you worry about that, baby.
Is it safe outside?

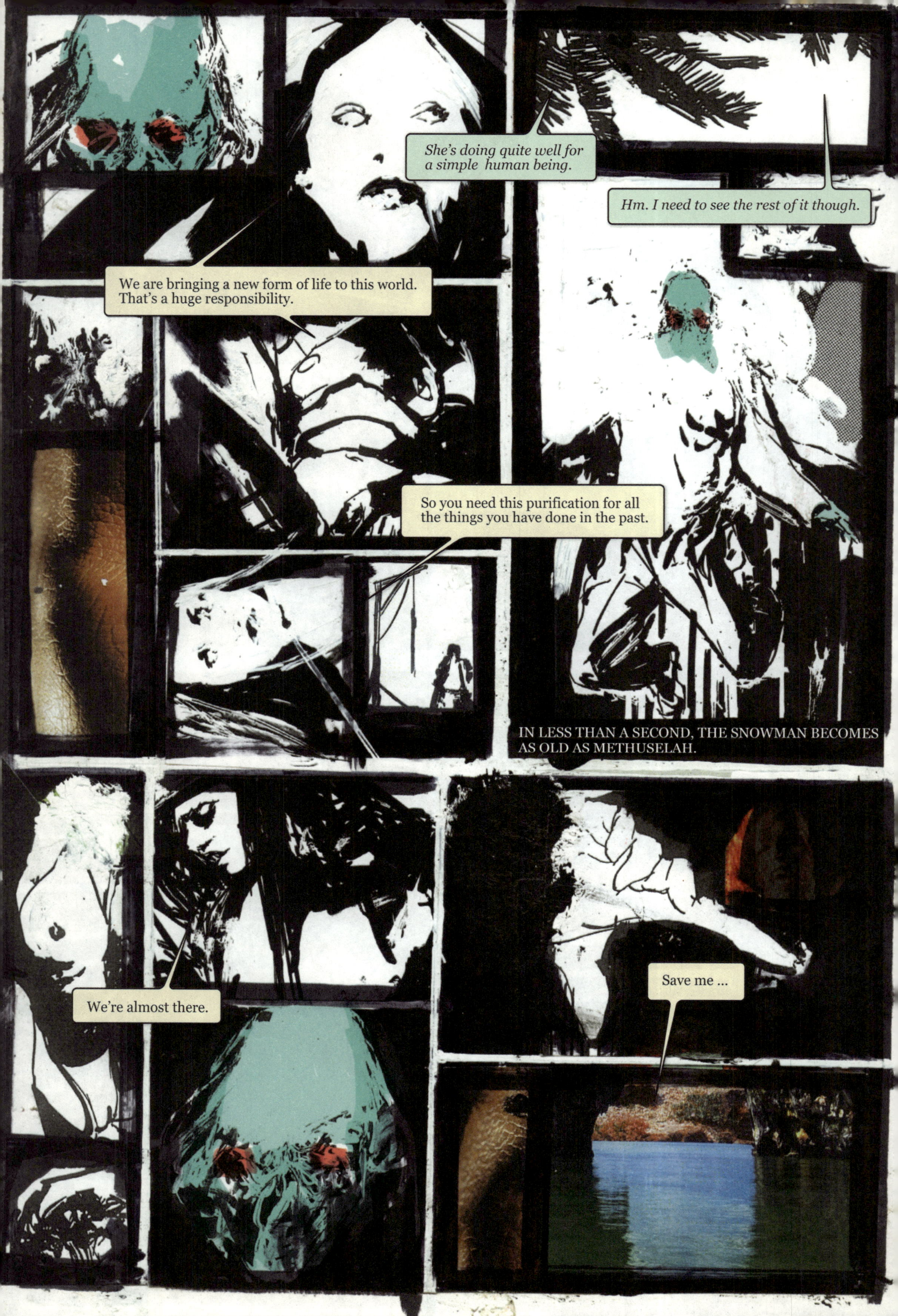

She's doing quite well for a simple human being.
Hm. I need to see the rest of it though.
We are bringing a new form of life to this world. That's a huge responsibility.
So you need this purification for all the things you have done in the past.
IN LESS THAN A SECOND, THE SNOWMAN BECOMES AS OLD AS METHUSELAH.
We're almost there.
Save me ...

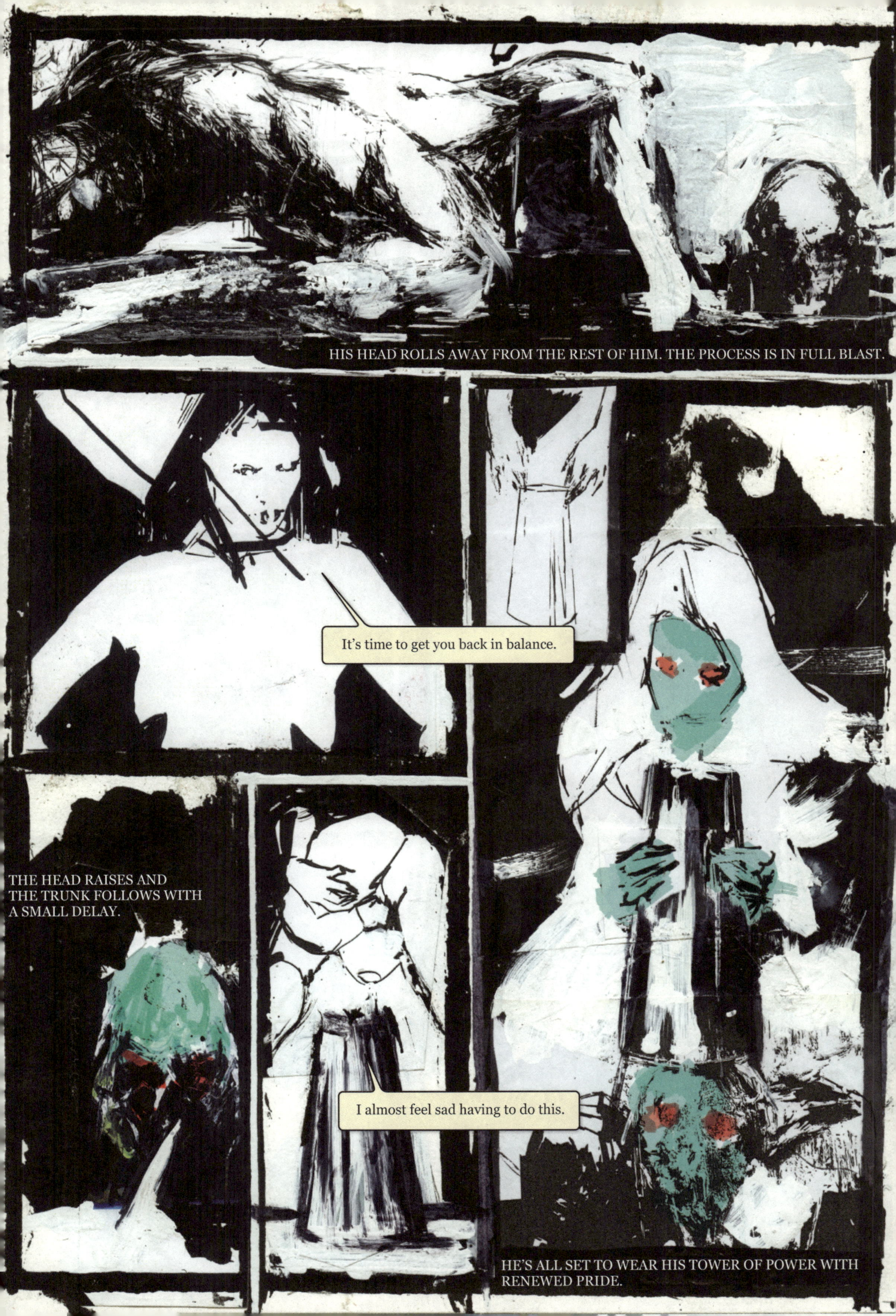

HIS HEAD ROLLS AWAY FROM THE REST OF HIM. THE PROCESS IS IN FULL BLAST.
It's time to get you back in balance.
THE HEAD RAISES AND THE TRUNK FOLLOWS WITH A SMALL DELAY.
I almost feel sad having to do this.
HE'S ALL SET TO WEAR HIS TOWER OF POWER WITH RENEWED PRIDE.

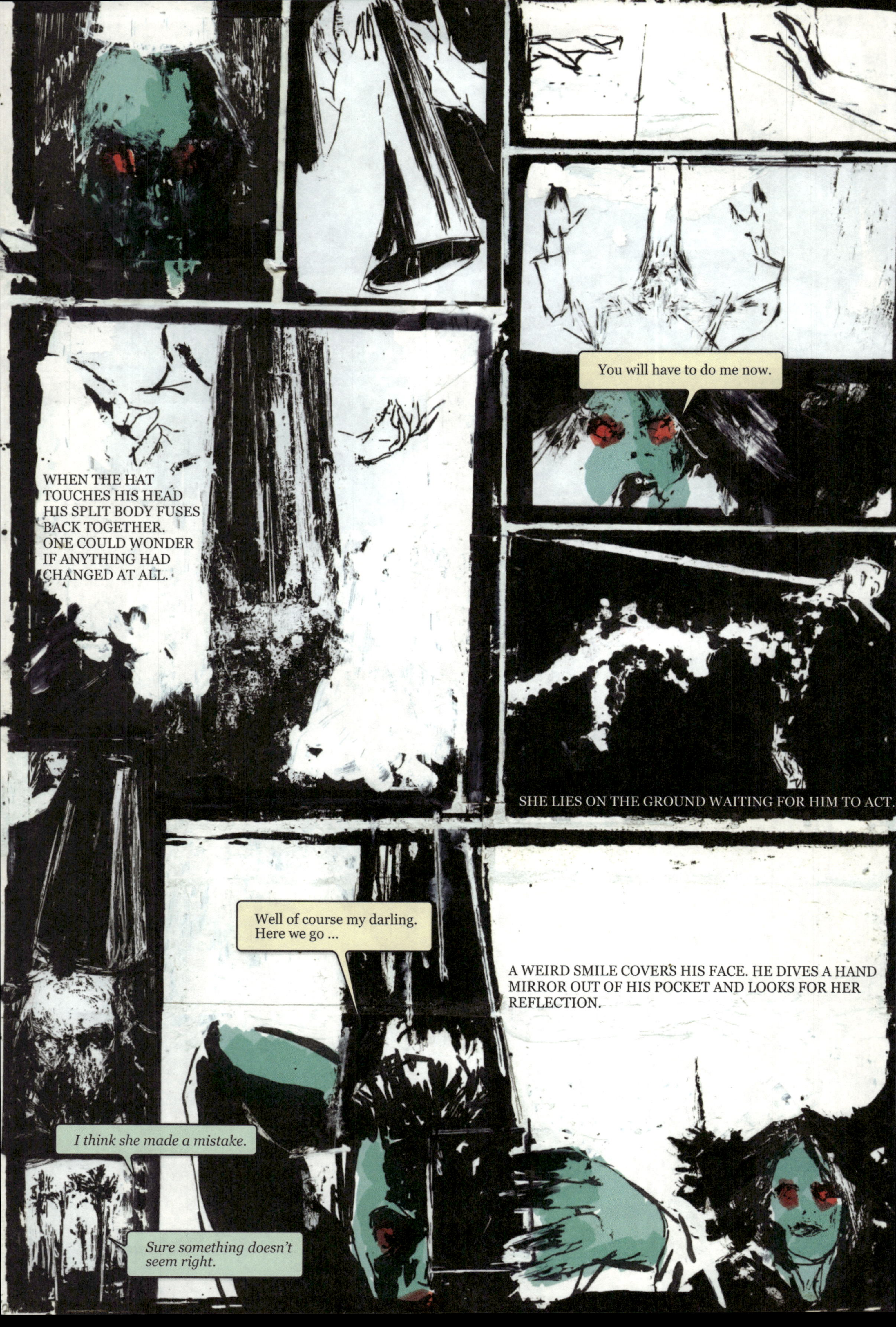
You will have to do me now.

WHEN THE HAT
TOUCHES HIS HEAD
HIS SPLIT BODY FUSES
BACK TOGETHER.
ONE COULD WONDER
IF ANYTHING HAD
CHANGED AT ALL.

SHE LIES ON THE GROUND WAITING FOR HIM TO ACT.

Well of course my darling.
Here we go ...

A WEIRD SMILE COVERS HIS FACE. HE DIVES A HAND
MIRROR OUT OF HIS POCKET AND LOOKS FOR HER
REFLECTION.

I think she made a mistake.

Sure something doesn't
seem right.

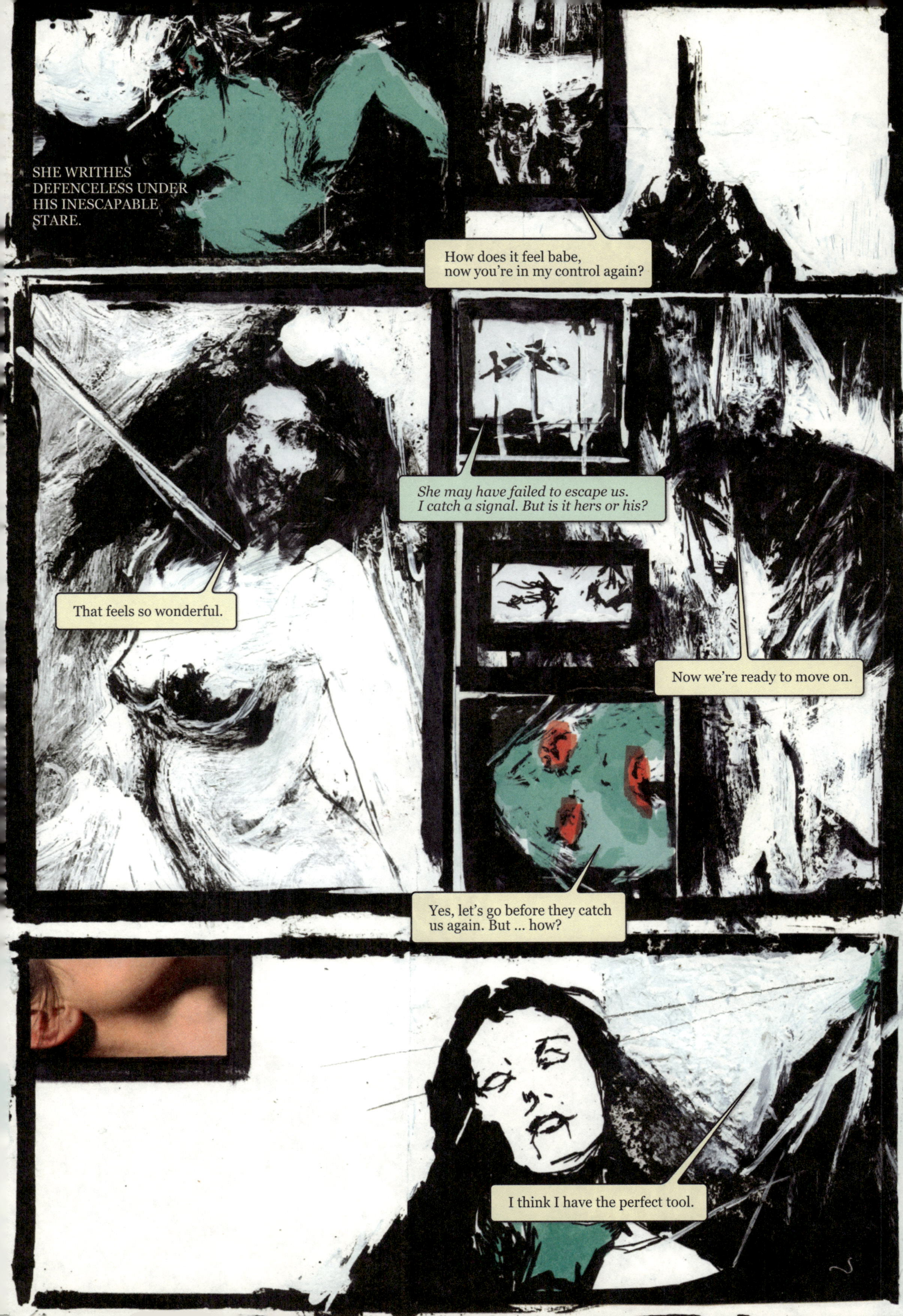

SHE WRITHES DEFENCELESS UNDER HIS INESCAPABLE STARE.
How does it feel babe, now you're in my control again?
That feels so wonderful.
She may have failed to escape us. I catch a signal. But is it hers or his?
Now we're ready to move on.
Yes, let's go before they catch us again. But ... how?
I think I have the perfect tool.

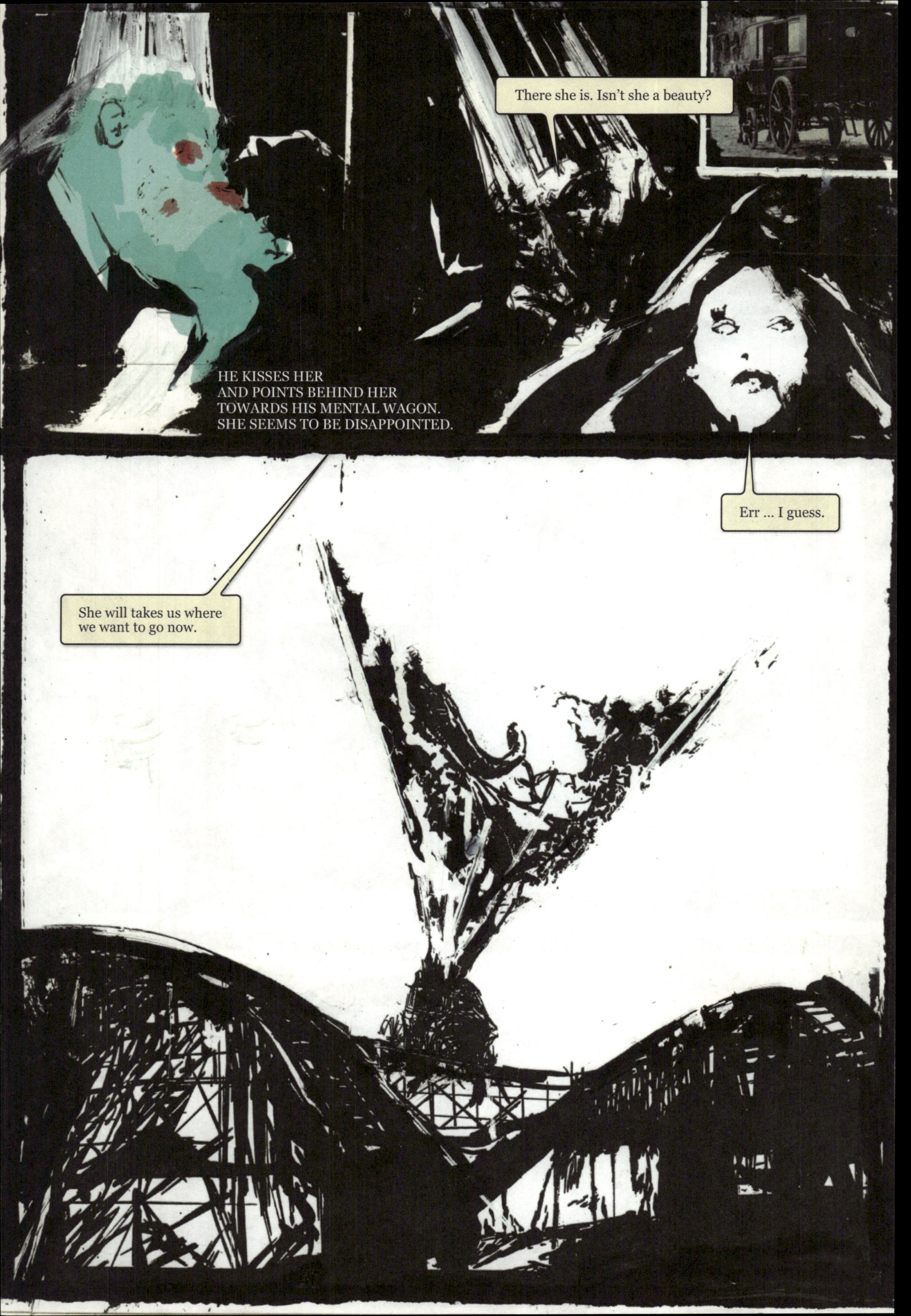

There she is. Isn't she a beauty?
HE KISSES HER
AND POINTS BEHIND HER
TOWARDS HIS MENTAL WAGON.
SHE SEEMS TO BE DISAPPOINTED.
Err ... I guess.
She will takes us where
we want to go now.

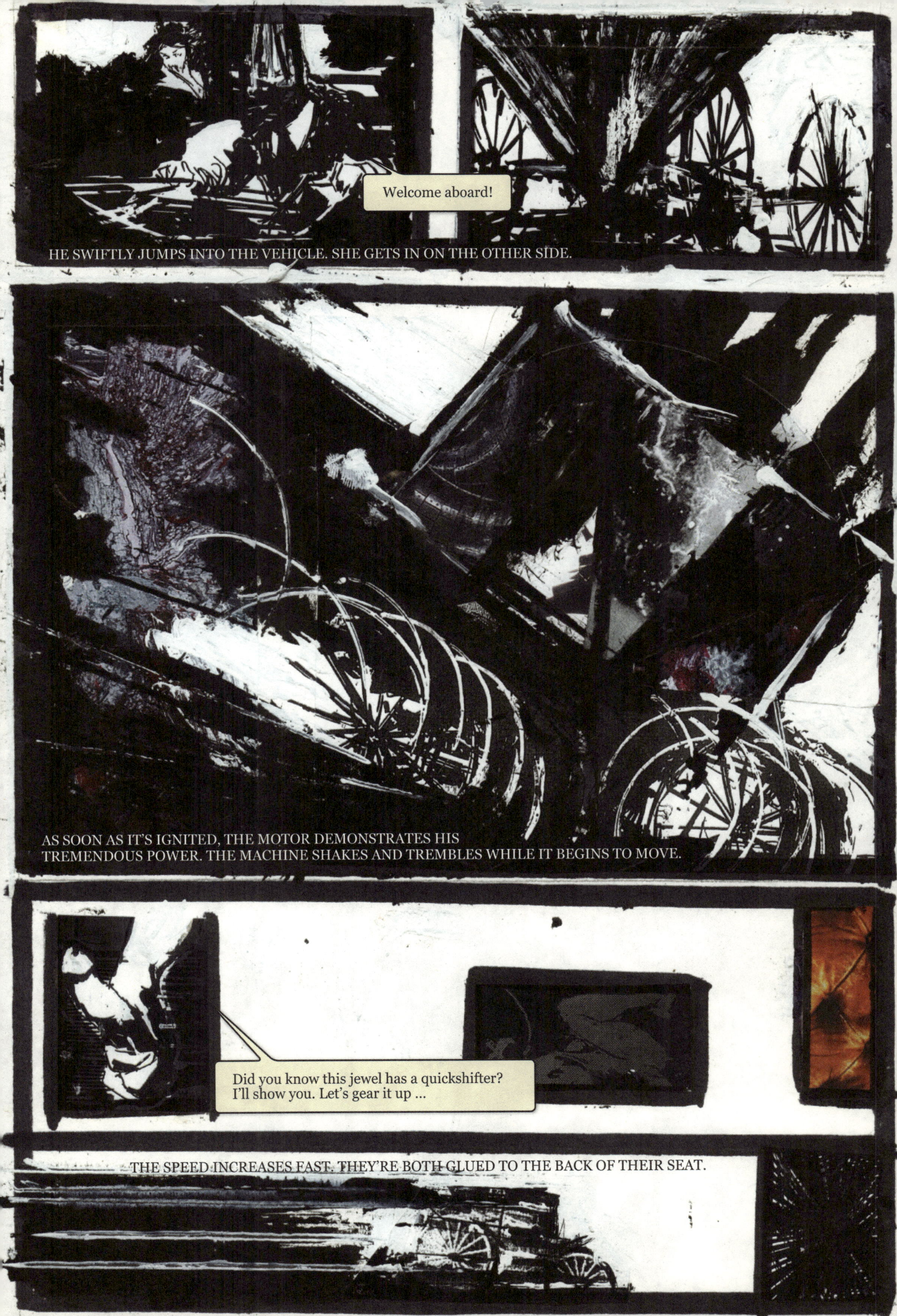

HE SWIFTLY JUMPS INTO THE VEHICLE. SHE GETS IN ON THE OTHER SIDE.

AS SOON AS IT'S IGNITED, THE MOTOR DEMONSTRATES HIS
TREMENDOUS POWER. THE MACHINE SHAKES AND TREMBLES WHILE IT BEGINS TO MOVE.

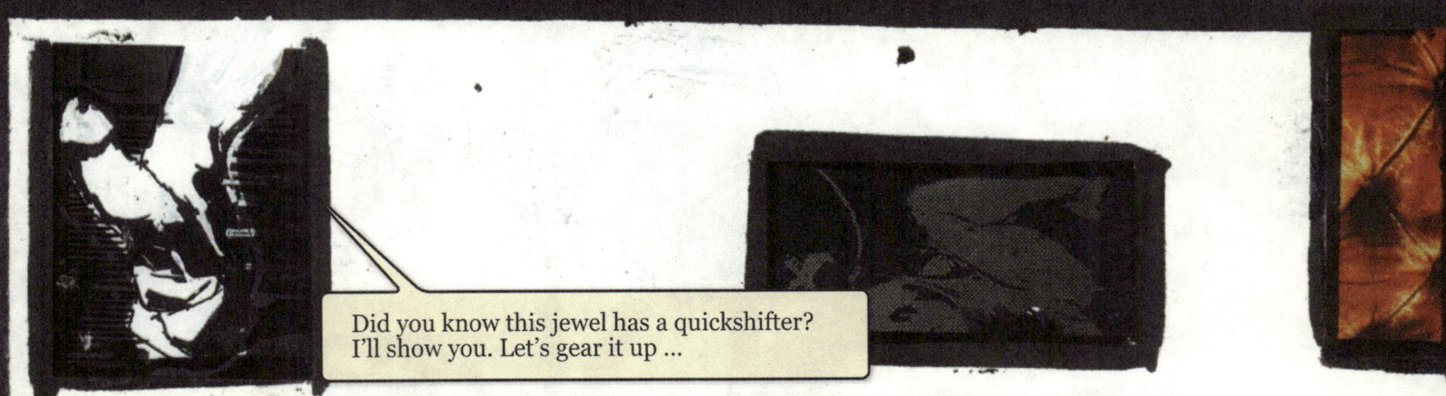

THE SPEED INCREASES FAST. THEY'RE BOTH GLUED TO THE BACK OF THEIR SEAT.

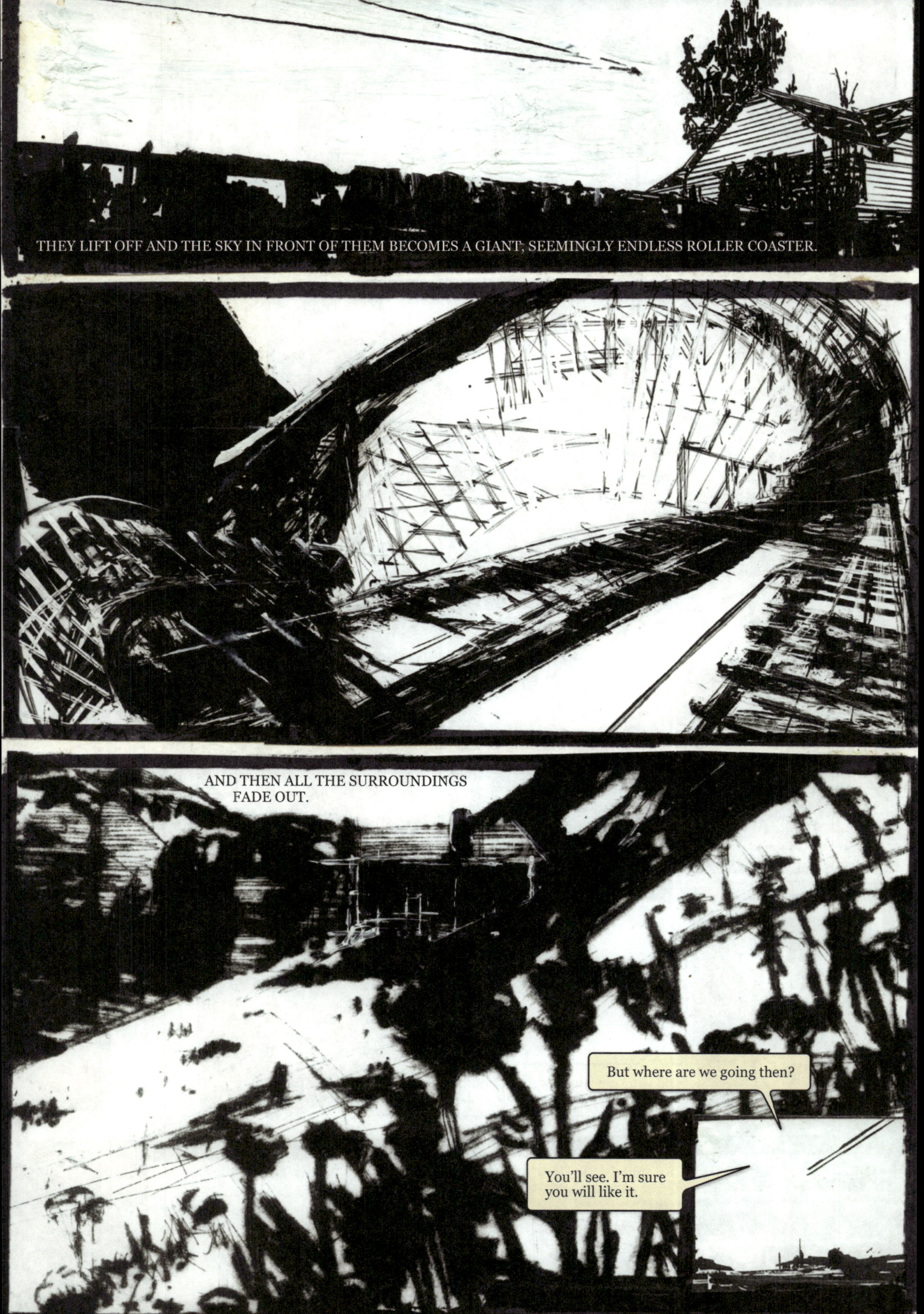

THEY LIFT OFF AND THE SKY IN FRONT OF THEM BECOMES A GIANT, SEEMINGLY ENDLESS ROLLER COASTER.
AND THEN ALL THE SURROUNDINGS FADE OUT.
But where are we going then?
You'll see. I'm sure you will like it.

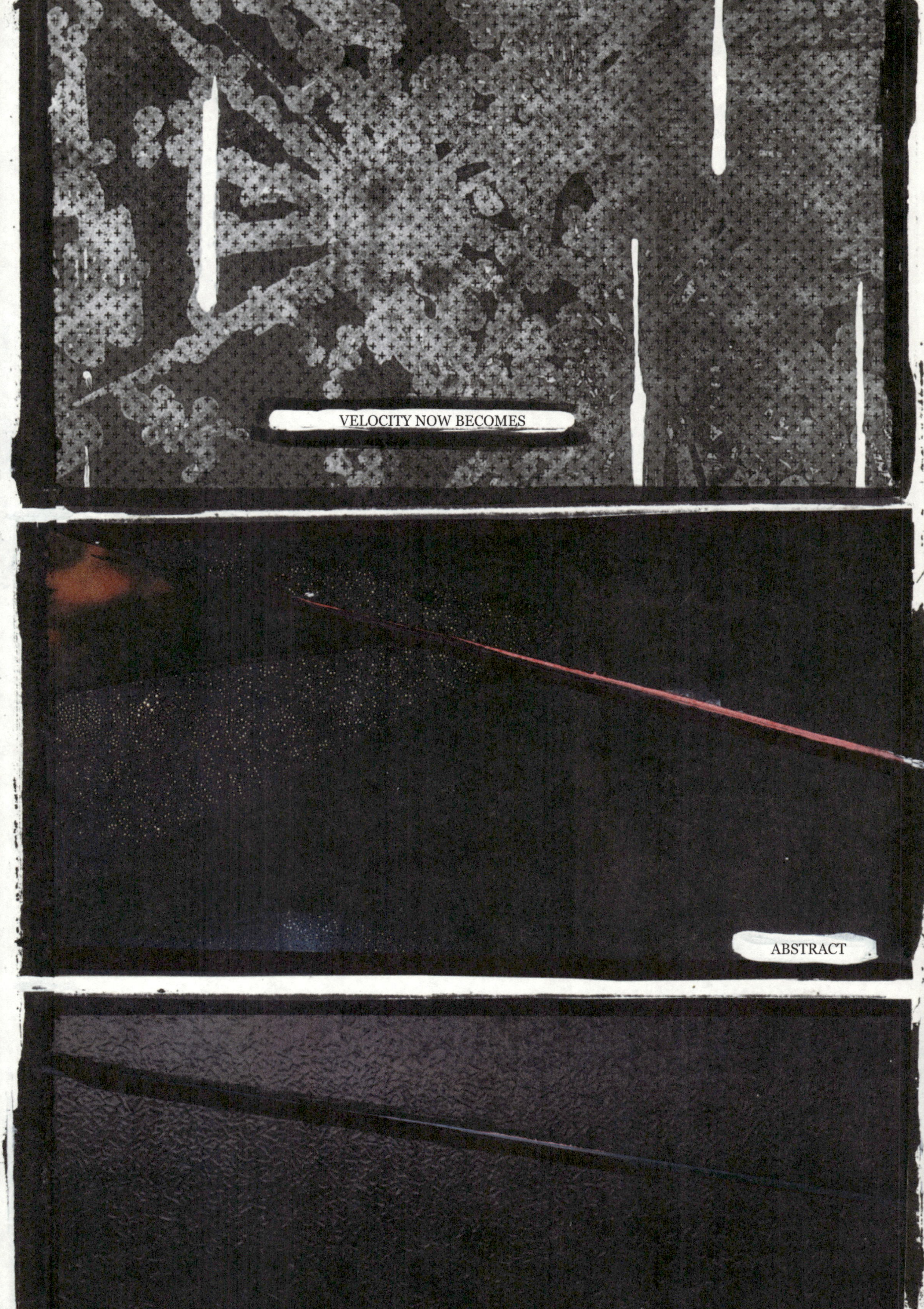
VELOCITY NOW BECOMES
ABSTRACT

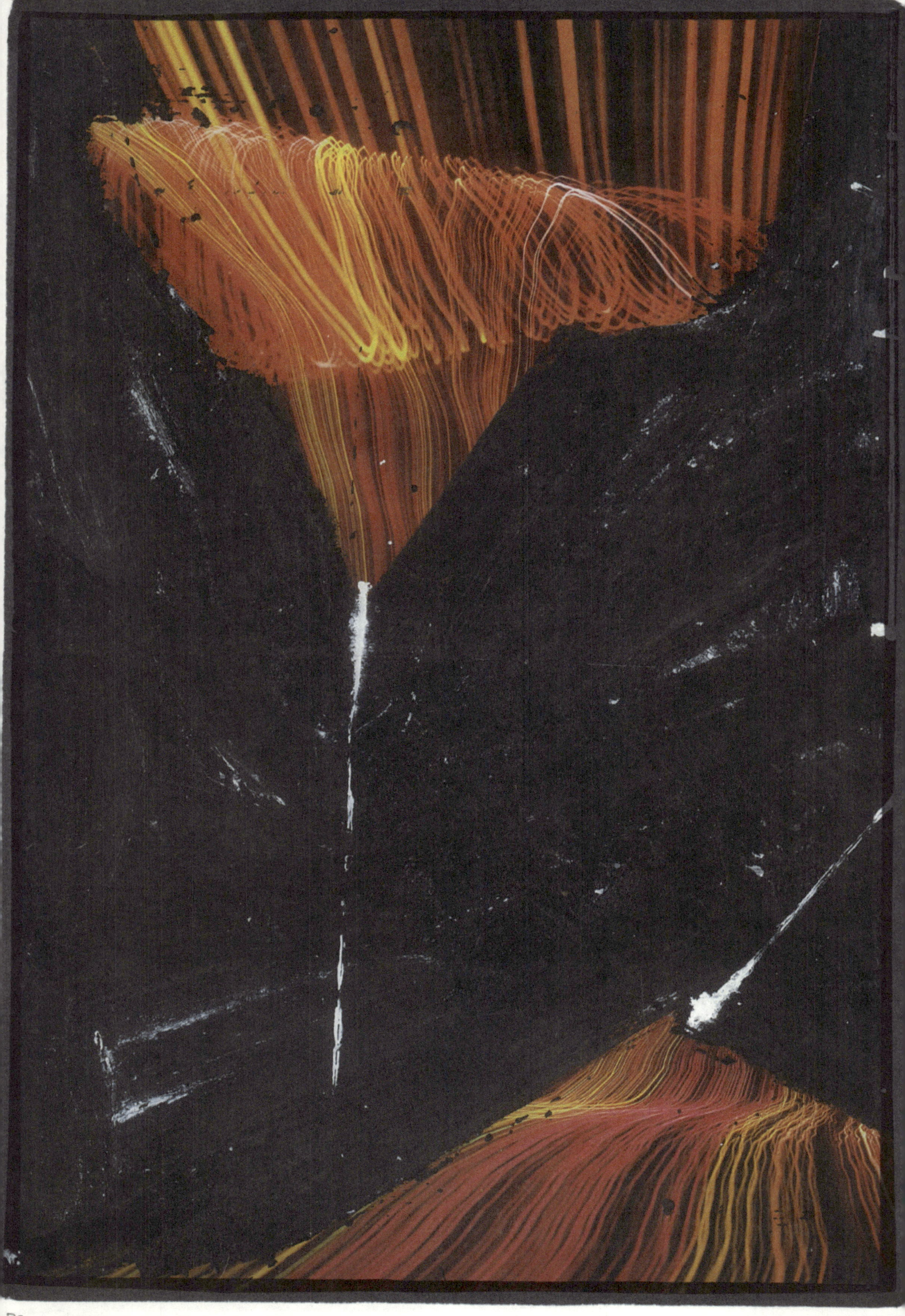

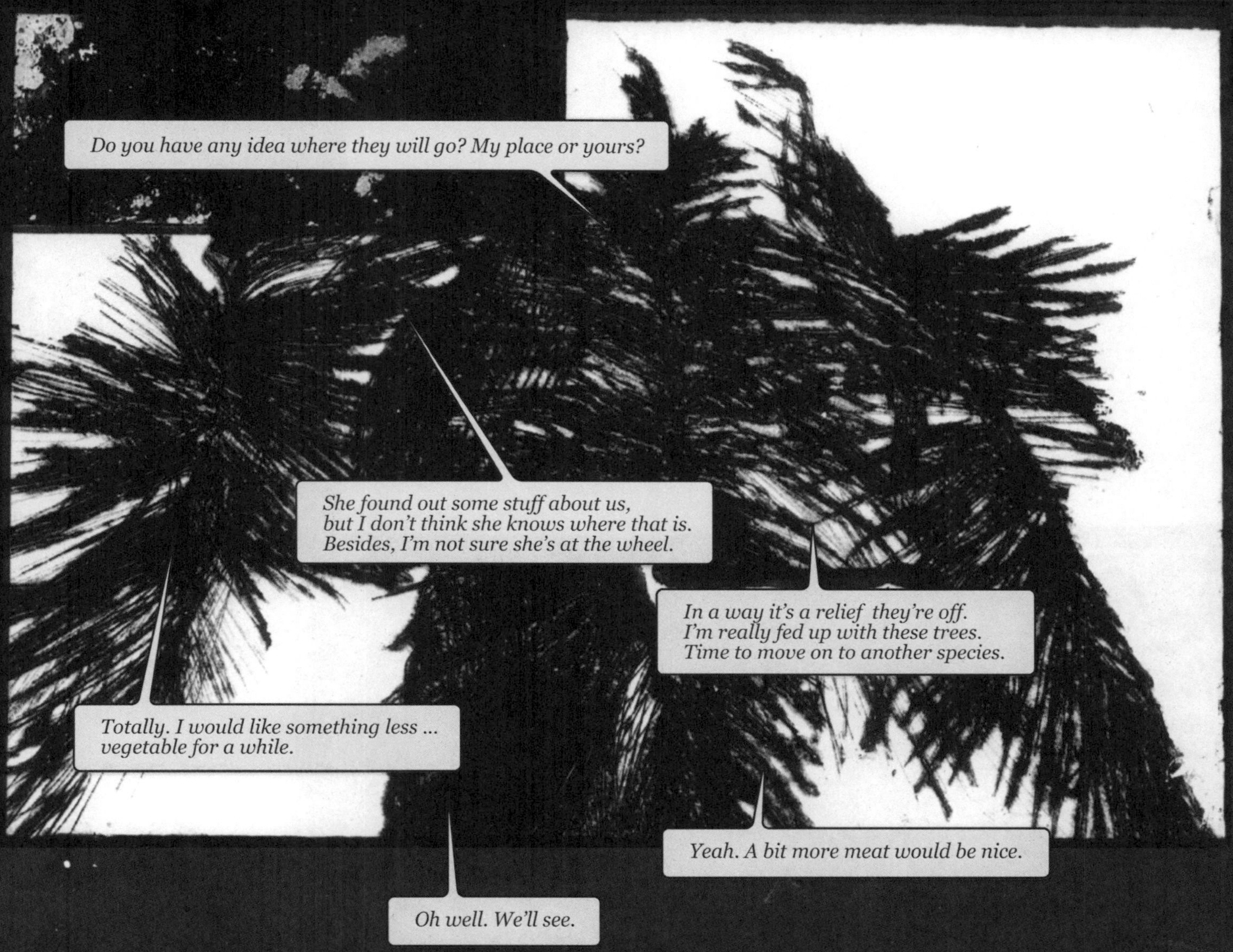

(CONTINUED IN PART 2)